AWAITING
the SONSHIP

JOEL BUTLER

Copyright © 2024 Joel Butler.

All rights reserved. No part of this book may be reproduced, stored, or transmitted by any means—whether auditory, graphic, mechanical, or electronic—without written permission of both publisher and author, except in the case of brief excerpts used in critical articles and reviews. Unauthorized reproduction of any part of this work is illegal and is punishable by law.

ISBN: 979-8-89419-097-6 (sc)
ISBN: 979-8-89419-098-3 (hc)
ISBN: 979-8-89419-099-0 (e)

Because of the dynamic nature of the Internet, any web addresses or links contained in this book may have changed since publication and may no longer be valid. The views expressed in this work are solely those of the author and do not necessarily reflect the views of the publisher, and the publisher hereby disclaims any responsibility for them.

One Galleria Blvd., Suite 1900, Metairie, LA 70001
(504) 702-6708

CONTENTS

Preface 1

Prologue 5

Chapter 1   The Entrance of Sin and Death 11

Chapter 2   Christ's Identification with Humanity 34

Chapter 3   The Identification of Humanity with Christ.... 55

Chapter 4   The Manifestation of the Sons of God............. 81

Chapter 5   The Glorious Liberty of the Children of God 118

Chapter 6   The Redemption of Our Bodies.......................150

Chapter 7   Sons of Adam/Adam's Death
             Sons of God/The Death of Christ....................172

Chapter 8   The Departure of Sin and Death 196

Epilogue...215

Appendix: Words of Unity in Paul's Letters.........................217

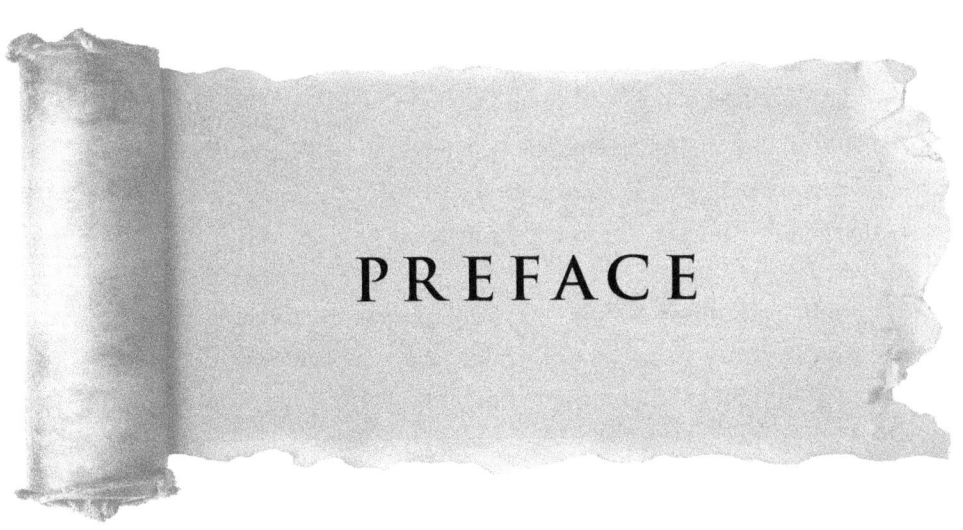

PREFACE

Over 2,000 years have transpired since Jesus ascended to the Father. As the glory of His promised return approaches nearer day by day, many believers today yearn for His appearing, embracing an increasing sense of hope while world events align with prophecy, signifying its certainty.

Paul, the apostle to the Gentile nations, terms the event associated with the return of Christ as the manifestation of the sons of God. Paul describes this unique occurrence in his letter to the Romans, specifically in chapter 8, verse 19.

This manuscript searches Paul's letters to the churches he founded in the first century to examine details related to this unprecedented occasion. Those who anticipate the incident should prepare themselves by reading and studying Paul's words that characterize the magnificent glory of His appearing.

"Awaiting the Sonship" is offered as an aid to Paul's solemn advice for proper preparation.

On a parallel course of action, God's adversary, the Prince of Darkness, will present to the world a counterfeit manifestation that will transpire during the same period. The description of this false appearance is also clearly defined in Paul's letters to the churches.

In the form of a wonder-working man speaking peace and prosperity, the imposter will stealthily enter the world stage. A strong delusion will subject the masses of humanity to lure the nations into worshiping a false Christ through a deceptive façade.

Enthralled by his extraordinary powers of persuasion, the nations of the world will embrace the scheming deceiver in the same manner as the original couple heeded the enticing advice of the subtle serpent in the Garden. Once the nations of the world embrace his wondrous works and words, they will be unable to turn away before the mask of deceit is removed.

Having come full circle on the wheel of history, the adversary will return to the larger garden of earth's domain to lure the unsuspecting human family of Adam and Eve into total slavery in his dark kingdom. He was successful once before in separating Eden's couple from God, and now, with greater power of seduction, he fully believes himself capable of capturing God's entire creation through fallen man for the final time.

During the interim period, prior to the exposure of the master deceiver, Christ will return for His body of believers. He will initiate the unification of the New Humanity, which He is creating in Himself. The New Creation process, which began in spirit with the Lord's sacrificial death and resurrection, is faithfully reported in the apostle Paul's letters.

Jesus has won the victory over the enemy of God long before the worldwide enchantment begins. Now, believers in His saving work are to be sealed from spell-binding sorcery. This protection is only possible through the gospel truths that Paul proclaimed. Faith in the saving work of Christ is provided through the protective armor of God in Paul's letters.

Paul's gospel is the source of truth, which produces a cohesive bond of God's peace and love, nourishing His body in waiting. The church, in preparing for Christ's appearing, must seek the divine wisdom of Paul's letters that adequately prepare believers to wage spiritual warfare.

The interruption of what began eons ago in the garden of God, between the Creator and the creature of His image, occurred in its initial stage. It was not by happenstance, but rather part of a divine plan that appeared to have been thwarted yet was only just beginning to advance.

God's plan for creation unfolds in Genesis, the first book of scripture. Throughout the Old Testament, Israel, the nation chosen by God to receive His oracles, appears to fail in its involvement. But God has not abandoned Israel, His chosen Son of the nations.

The New Testament begins the process of redemption for Adam's family, the first man from whom all humans find their source of natural life. Adam's disobedience to God brought forth both sin and death into the creation, affecting the relationship with God and causing estrangement between the Creator and mankind.

Humanity was not the only affected part of the old creation; the entire universe came under the destructive effects of Adam's disobedience.

Jesus Christ, the Son of the Living God, came to earth during his first appearance to reclaim humanity by means of his obedience to God, whom Jesus referred to as his Father. Upon His return, Jesus will release the universe from the vanity it was placed under by the transgression of Adam.

Both Israel and the true church, the Body of Christ, will fulfill their respective roles in the next era and beyond.

"Awaiting the Sonship" is intended to enlighten the readers as to Christ's accomplishments and prepare them for the imminent return of their Savior.

PROLOGUE

For as many as are led by the Spirit of God, they are the sons of God.

For ye have not received the spirit of bondage again to fear; but ye have received the Spirit of adoption, whereby we cry, Abba, Father.

The Spirit itself beareth witness with our spirit, that we are the children of God: And if children, then heirs; heirs of God, and jointheirs with Christ; if so be that we suffer with him, that we may be also glorified together.

For I reckon that the sufferings of this present time are not worthy to be compared with the glory which shall be revealed in us.

For the earnest expectation of the creature waiteth for the manifestation of the sons of God.

For the creature was made subject to vanity, not willingly, but by reason of him who hath subjected the same in hope, Because the creature itself also shall be delivered from the bondage of corruption into the glorious liberty of the children of God.

> *For we know that the whole creation groaneth and travaileth in pain together until now. And not only they, but ourselves also, which have the firstfruits of the Spirit, even we ourselves groan within ourselves, waiting for the adoption, to wit, the redemption of our body.*
>
> *For we are saved by hope: but hope that is seen is not hope:*
>
> *for what a man seeth, why doth he yet hope for? But if we hope for that we see not, then do we with patience wait for it. Romans 8:18-25, KJV*

The Body of Christ awaits an occurrence that will far surpass anything previously experienced or imagined. The Body of Christ's believing family will be transformed and then transferred into an entirely new realm.

The anticipated event is the *huiosthesia (Romans 8:23)*, which is the placing of God's sons into face-to-face service with the Master, whom at present is served by the members of the Body in *newness of spirit (Romans 7:6)*.

When joined with Jesus in the finalization of God's plan for this era and the ages to follow, those that belong to Him will be clothed with a new body fashioned to be like His body *(Philippians 3:20–21)*. Currently, an inward transformation in spirit is causing a new perspective that is attuned to a spiritual mindset. When He returns, the outward body will conform to the inward man of the heart.

Under the new covenant, the nation of Israel will also experience conversion. Israel will realize that the divine service promised to them has been held in abeyance until the proper time in God's plan. Jesus is approaching on the near horizon. As their promised Messiah, He will restore the kingdom and set in place their ministry to the nations. But their renewal is not an isolated event.

The elements and the orderly system of the first creation fell into a state of degradation and corruption when Adam and his mate believed the lie of the adversary and disobeyed their Creator. God had adequately warned the first man of the consequences of disobedience.

The revolutionary changes initiated by the son-placing (sonship) events will result in the complete reversal of creation's vanity through the freedom of God's children. The creation's release will alter the damaging and destructive effects of universal slavery on both sin and death.

The next phase of Christ's saving work will begin with the nullification of both sin and death. The saving work of Christ is a continual process of renewal.

In this current era, His victory is expressed through faith in Him, both in His words and in His work. Those who are blessed by the divine gift of persuasion become members of His body. They know of the Creator's ability and determination to complete all the work He has sent His Son to do, beginning with Christ's crucifixion, death, burial, and resurrection.

His victory is being expressed through His Son's body, the true church. The renewed nation of Israel will embrace His victory when they are grafted back into the tree of service from which they were once cut out (Romans 11:23).

During the ensuing ages, the evil domination of all ungodly authority, principalities, rule, and dominion that oppose God's divine plan in the first creation will be defeated and placed under Christ Jesus' feet.

> *For this purpose, the Son of God was manifested, that he might destroy the works of the devil. I John 3:8b*

This is the blessed hope of the Body of Christ, Israel, and the glorious expectation of the Creation. It is also the answer to His early disciples, who, before His ascension, earnestly asked their master if Israel's restoration was to occur without delay.

The Kingdom of Christ was to be entered first by the called-out assembly of the Jewish disciples and the Gentile nations through Paul's ministry. The kingdom began to be expressed in the innermost new man of the heart. Then, the visible kingdom will be administered on earth by the reborn nation of Israel. Their Messiah, Jesus, the Son of Man, will return on His second advent. The ministry of the sons of God, under the direction of Christ, will subdue the enemies of God as the consummation is attained.

> *Then cometh the end, when he shall have delivered up the kingdom to God, even the Father; when he shall have put down all rule and all authority and power.*
>
> *25 For he must reign, till he hath put all enemies under his feet.*
>
> *26 The last enemy that shall be destroyed is death.*
>
> *27 For he hath put all things under his feet. But when he saith all things are put under him, it is manifest that he is excepted, which did put all things under him.*
>
> *28 And when all things shall be subdued unto him, then shall the Son also himself be subject unto him that put all things under him, that God may be all in all. I Corinthians 15:24-28*

Christ's return for His body will inaugurate the unification of the New Humanity, which began in spirit in the Lord's sacrificial death and resurrection, as faithfully reported through the apostle Paul's ministry.

Paul's gospel is the catalyst for producing the cohesive bond of His peace and love necessary for His body in waiting, the church, to prepare for His appearing. Many may claim that the church is in decline, but the Spirit of God testifies otherwise.

Awaiting the Sonship is expressed in the following pages with a view to kindling a fervent hope and desire for the return of the Master, the King of kings and the Lord of lords.

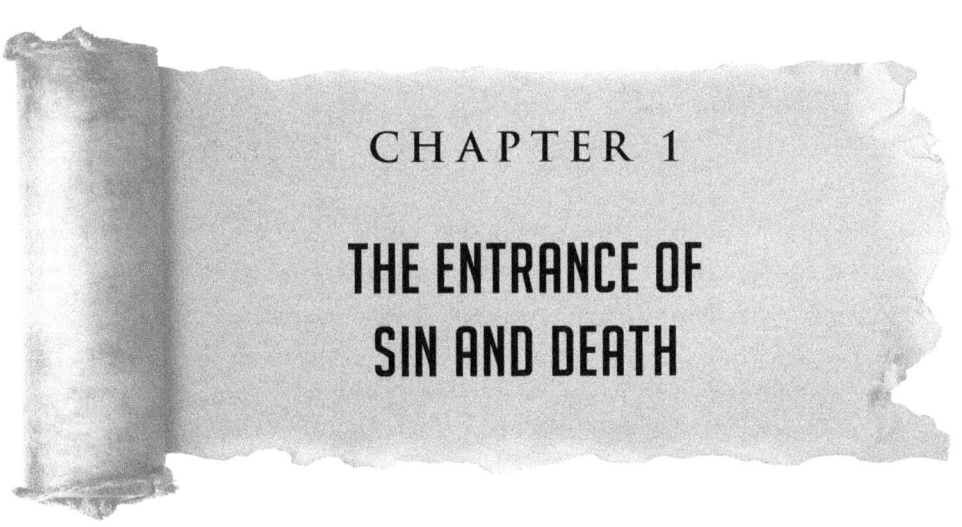

CHAPTER 1

THE ENTRANCE OF SIN AND DEATH

THE BEGINNING OF GOD'S PLAN

God's plan to create and fashion mankind in His image was interrupted in its initial stage. Surely not by happenstance, man's fall from grace and separation were part of a divine plan that appeared to have been thwarted but was only beginning to unfold.

Adam, the first human, was unified with God when placed in the garden. Additionally, Adam was unified with Eve, the woman who was taken out of him and formed from part of his body, to serve as his helper in their work.

They, as a united couple of one flesh, were spiritually joined with their creator until the subtle serpent entered and deceived Eve. She became linked to the serpent's lie as he enticed her to eat the fruit of the tree of the knowledge of good and evil. Exactly as the Lord God had warned Adam, their disobedience resulted in death as an apparent permanent separation from their relationship with their Creator.

The serpent's subtle deceit led to direct opposition with God through the lie that they would not die, as God had warned, but would become wise like God, knowing good from evil. The result is what is commonly known as the "fall" of humanity. They became dying sinners and enemies of God by siding with God's chief adversary, the serpent.

When Eve coaxed her mate into joining her in the defection, they both began to die when Adam ate the forbidden fruit. The dying process eventually culminated in their entry into the state of death.

At death, the human spirit is separated from the body to return to the heavenlies, from whence it came to the Father of all spirits (Hebrews 12:9). Jesus described this moment of death as when His spirit and His body were separated.

> *When Jesus therefore had received the vinegar, he said, It is finished: and he bowed his head, and gave up the ghost. John 19:30*

Upon death, the physical body returns to the dust from which it came. Upon death, the soul separates from the body and returns to the unseen, or imperceptible, from which it came. It will remain unexpressive in that mode until the spirit is again joined to the body.

Death is both a return and a separation. Resurrection is a reunion, a rejoining of the constituent parts.

Human life is a joint relationship between God and humanity. God is the source of life. It is a union between the Creator and the created. As long as the spirit, soul, and body remain joined, the human possesses *bios (Strong's #G979, the present state of existence)*.

In the garden, before the serpent practiced his dark deceit, God and the human couple enjoyed close companionship. However, their fellowship was not continual in that God would separate Himself periodically from Adam and Eve, returning to the garden in the cool of the day (Genesis 3:8).

God's temporary absence provided a surreptitious opportunity for the serpent to enter the garden, seeking to draw the couple away from their Creator. The schemer exercised the wiles of his covertly clandestine nature. As the father of lies, in whom there is no truth, his diabolical treachery succeeded.

Jesus described the nature of the adversary when He spoke to the Pharisees, asserting that they were the enemy's children and not children of God, as they claimed.

> *Ye are of your father the devil, and the lusts of your father ye will do. He was a murderer from the beginning, and abode not in the truth, because there is no truth in him. When he speaketh a lie, he speaketh of his own: for he is a liar, and the father of it. John 8:44*

As reported in Genesis 3, when the Creator returned to the Garden, as His unfaithful children had been duped by the foe, He executed judgment upon the serpent, the man, and the woman for the transgression. He sent the man and his mate from the garden, now fallen in sin, separating the couple from the tree of life. The serpent had accomplished the entry of sin and the resultant ration of death through Adam, affecting the entire human race as well as the entire creation.

The offense of the chosen couple not only affected all other humans, who would come out of Adam and through Eve, but would adversely impact the universe. God's fallen family on earth and the entire first creation suffer from the bondage of the despotic rule of its new master, the god of this world (II Corinthians 4:4).

God will end humanity's estrangement, as the separation is temporary and their reunion is inevitable. God turns evil into good. This testimony is confirmed throughout scripture.

Before the narrative of Genesis closes, the story of Joseph, Jacob's favorite son, serves as a perfect example of God's mercy and blessing.

Joseph was a man who interpreted dreams, which began with his own personal dreams as he recited them to his jealous brothers. They hated Joseph without cause and betrayed him. At first, when they sought to kill him because of his dreams, they were dissuaded and sold him to traveling merchants, who, in turn, sold him into slavery in Egypt. Joseph's victorious life while in Egypt provides a view of God's triumphant love.

Joseph, betrayed by his brothers due to their hatred towards his favored status with their common father, was once again reunited with them and with his father, Jacob. Upon Jacob's death, the reunified band of brothers carried his bones from Egypt, burying him in Canaan as Jacob once instructed. The heartfelt exchange between them reveals a solemn truth concerning good and evil and the overcoming power of the love of God.

> *And when Joseph's brethren saw that their father was dead, they said, Joseph will peradventure hate us, and will certainly requite us all the evil which we did unto him.*
>
> *And they sent a messenger unto Joseph, saying, thy father did command before he died, saying,*
>
> *So shall ye say unto Joseph, Forgive, I pray thee now, the trespass of thy brethren, and their sin; for they did unto thee evil: and now, we pray thee, forgive the trespass of the servants of the God of thy father. And Joseph wept when they spake unto him.*
>
> *And his brethren went and fell down before his face; and they said, Behold, we be thy servants.*

> *And Joseph said unto them, Fear not: for am I in the place of God?*
>
> *But as for you, ye thought evil against me; but God meant it unto good, to bring to pass, as it is this day, to save much people alive. Genesis 50:15-20*

God uses evil to bring about salvation, recovery, and reunion.

Sin leads to redemption. The evil of the enemy will be the catalyst used by God to ultimately glorify Himself in the work of salvation for all humanity through His only begotten Son.

Both sin and death will be removed.

The God of Love will accomplish His grand and glorious goal, being fully joined to the New Humanity, as He will be worshiped and adored by a joyful, grateful family as numerous as the stars in the sky and the sand of the seas.

As Paul instructed the church in Rome, his words seem impossible to the flesh, but with the New Man's obedience in response to God's overwhelming love, Jesus can transform evil into good.

> *Therefore, if thine enemy hunger, feed him; if he thirsts, give him drink: for in so doing thou shalt heap coals of fire on his head.*
>
> *Be not overcome of evil but overcome evil with good. Romans 12:20-21*

The goal of this manuscript is to discuss how the body of Christ, as members joined together with Christ, along with restored Israel, will be the blessing God originally planned. God, through Christ, will eliminate division. Reconciliation will end the separation.

As it is written;

> *For I am persuaded, that neither death, nor life, nor angels, nor principalities, nor powers, nor things present, nor things to come,*
>
> *Nor height, nor depth, nor any other creature, shall be able to separate us from the love of God, which is in Christ Jesus our Lord. Romans 8:38-39*

Mankind was created and formed in the image of God, demonstrating a likeness and resemblance to the maker of this unique creature. During the creation phase, both male and female members of humanity were designated as representative figures to be like God, who is specified in Genesis 1 as Elohim, a plural unity of divine ones, the Supreme Deity.

Thus, the heavens and the earth were finished, and all the host of them. (Genesis 2:1). Elohim finished the creation phase on the sixth day and rested on the seventh day from the work of the first six days, as described in Genesis 1. The heavens and the earth, and all of the host of them, were finished by the end of the sixth day. The word in Hebrew for "finished" is *kalah (Strong's #3615, meaning to end, to cease, to complete).* The word in the Hebrew for "host of them" is *tsaba (Strong's #6635, meaning a mass of persons, especially organized for war, an army).*

And on the seventh day God ended his work which he had made; and he rested on the seventh day from all his work which he had made (Genesis 2:2). The word used to specify that He ended his work is *kalah.* The word for "rested" is *shabath (Stong's #7673, meaning to cease, desist, or rest).*

When God concluded His creation work, He completed the entire human family. All persons to be brought forth on earth were first created as spiritual beings in the celestial realm. Each individual, along with all other persons, was created from God's spirit, as He is the Father of spirits (Hebrews 12:9).

It is fitting to note that the vast throng of humans is characterized as an army, suggesting a battle-ready force to wage war. It appears that God's initial creation would be the battleground in which the conflict and struggle between good and evil would occur. Sin and righteousness are locked in conflict, death and life as well, culminating in the virtuous battle of love overcoming evil.

Each person's human body is introduced by and through their human father of their flesh, a descendant of Adam, as initially created in the Genesis 1 account. Each person is a spirit housed in a human body, whose body has its source in Adam, the original man.

When the human spirit is joined with that person's earthly body, the human soul of that person is consciously alive and expressive (Genesis 2:7). The soul is that facet of mankind's being that is in the middle ground of the opposition between the flesh and the spirit. Flesh is from the earth; spirit is from heaven.

David described in poetic form the battle for the soul.

> *Unto thee, O Lord, do I lift up my soul.*
>
> *O my God, I trust in thee: let me not be ashamed, let not mine enemies triumph over me. Psalm 25:1-2*

As to the other wondrous parts of man, David, in Psalm 139, expressed the process of his formation in this manner:

> *For thou hast possessed my reins: thou hast covered me in my mother's womb.*
>
> *I will praise thee; for I am fearfully and wonderfully made: marvellous are thy works; and that my soul knoweth right well.*

> *My substance was not hid from thee, when I was made in secret, and curiously wrought in the lowest parts of the earth.*
>
> *Thine eyes did see my substance yet being imperfect; and in thy book all my members were written, which in continuance were fashioned, when as yet there was none of them.*
>
> *How precious also are thy thoughts unto me, O God! how great is the sum of them! Psalms 139:13-17*

Paul also revealed God's goal of conforming His children as Christ's brethren.

> *And we know that all things work together for good to them that love God, to them who are the called according to his purpose.*
>
> *For whom he did foreknow, he also did predestinate to be conformed to the image of his Son, that he might be the firstborn among many brethren.*
>
> *Moreover, whom he did predestinate, them he also called: and whom he called, them he also justified: and whom he justified, them he also glorified. Romans 8:28-30*

Paul reveals that God has detailed knowledge of each of us. Further, in a process of conformity, we are predetermined to reflect the image of God's Son. And further still, we will be jointly formed as brothers of Him, who is the firstborn. This conforming process will involve our calling, then our justification, and finally, our glorification.

God's goal of a huge family of adoring and thankful mature siblings will be accomplished within the eons that have been created for this purpose.

God knew every human before he was individually brought forth into the world through the human birth process. All humans are generated by the union of the human father and mother. The creator is the spiritual father who animates all creatures, finding their source of life in Him.

God also, according to the verses above from Paul, has a purpose for creating all things. He limits in advance, by predetermination, the boundaries of the lives of each of His creatures in order to conform each to the image of His Son. Each individual human is called forth when the Father determines at which point He will justify them and then glorify them.

On the earth, God separated the land from the waters, where the seeds of the plants and the herbs were to spring forth, but not until the Lord God caused rain to fall upon the earth. Until the rain came forth, a mist was upon the earth, providing moisture for initial growth. This was in anticipation of the Lord God introducing the human to the earth, the creature created in His image. (Genesis 2:5,6)

During the creation phase, God separated components from others to distinguish separate functions: the heavens and the earth, the stars in the heavens, the waters from above and below, the seas and the dry land, the different kinds of animals, beasts, birds, and creeping things. And on the sixth day of the week, He formed man out of the earth, separate from the beasts of the fields.

All was brought into existence as good, and humanity as very good.

Adam was the first human formed from the soil of the new earth. His physical earthen body encompassed bones for his framework, flesh to cover the structure, organs and blood to supply fuel for the operating mechanics of his uniquely wondrous physique. Then, upon God's completion of his physical vessel, man received the breath of life from his creator. When the breath of spirit and the body were united, Adam was empowered to observe, think, speak, and act as a living soul. (Genesis 2:7)

The first man was the prototype representative of all of humanity. All subsequent humans would be introduced into the world by Adam through human conception and birth. No other human would be formed directly from the soil, as was Adam. Through Adam, whose body was made of soil, all humans would become living souls resident in bodies of flesh from the soil of the earth, empowered by the life of the spirit.

In that initial physical life in the garden where he had been placed, Adam enjoyed fellowship with the Lord God, from whom he would receive guidance and training. Accordingly, the Lord God instructed him, as to his physical work, to dress and keep the garden. God also instructed Adam as to the nutrition plan to sustain the ongoing tasks of his service in the garden.

Adam was the original man of the earth. He was a solitary being, relating to his creator when they enjoyed fellowship together. During that early phase, Adam was unaware of his need to be joined by another human as his complement.

> *And the Lord God said, It is not good that the man should be alone; I will make him an help meet for him. Genesis 2:18*

This was the first occasion that the Lord God described the circumstances of His creation as *"not good."* An insight into God's heart is provided in these words. God did not create us as solitary creatures. It is vital that we have companions that help us, build us up, and complete us.

Unknown to Adam at that time, all succeeding physical vessels of humanity would be born deriving their humanity from Adam. The Lord God took Eve out of Adam while he was put to sleep in a divine operation. The Lord God took a part of Adam's body, then intricately fashioned the woman as man's helper. She, like him, is a spirit being placed into her physical body, becoming a living soul.

The male seed originating in Adam would unite with the female ovum as their counterparts through the process of generation. They would inaugurate the propagation of the human family upon the earth in response to the Lord God's mandate to be fruitful and multiply (Genesis 1:28).

A woman, the female counterpart to the man, would complement her mate. She would complete him by reproducing an entire human family, all created in God's image, all originating in Adam in bodily form, and passing through her into the inhabited earth.

Every human individual is a creature of three parts: spirit, soul, and body (I Thessalonians 5:23).

As Adam's complement, the woman would assist the man in fulfilling his duties before God. As fashioned from a part of him, she would function together with him, utilizing and displaying the divine gifts that prepared her to be an adequate aid to the man. They would act together as joint tenants of the garden, serving God and worshipping Him through their service.

Adam would serve God by cultivating the garden.

Eve would serve God by utilizing her gifts to discern threats to the garden. In her capacity as helpmeet, which comes from a root word describing protection, she would "keep" or protect the garden as Adam cultivated the soil.

The initial conversation between Adam and the Lord God before Eve was brought forth occurred in Genesis 2:16–17, as follows:

> *[16] And the Lord God commanded the man, saying, Of every tree of the garden thou mayest freely eat:*

> *¹⁷But of the tree of the knowledge of good and evil, thou shalt not eat of it: for in the day that thou eatest thereof thou shalt surely die.*

This limited conversation between the Lord God and Adam focused on the abundance of fruit in the garden that Adam could eat. His instruction was full of grace, only limited by a single restraint. The Lord God gave one simple warning. Adam was not to eat of the tree of the knowledge of good and evil. Disobedience would cause his death.

There would be more, however, to the act of eating the fruit than introducing death, as Paul described in his letter to the Romans.

> *Wherefore, as by one man sin entered into the world, and death by sin; and so death passed upon all men, for that all have sinned: Romans 5:12*

Both sin and death entered into the creation through Adam's disobedience. Sin and death affect every human as well. The presence of both sin and death passing on through Adam causes every person to be a dying sinner.

Before the woman was taken out of the man, the Lord God provided Adam with the instructions. There is no evidence in the scripture narrative that Eve received the instructions concerning dietary matters directly from God. Because Adam was instructed by the Lord God and his mate was not privy to the first conversation, Adam was obviously her source of the Lord God's information and direction concerning their service to God.

There is no indication that Adam properly instructed her according to the exact directions that the Lord God instructed Adam. Although Eve was given to Adam as his complement, there is no indication of any dialogue between them regarding the fruit of the trees or any exchange of instructions in the garden.

Eve's knowledge of the instructions is discerned by the next conversation in the Garden, which in the Genesis narrative occurs between the serpent, the most subtle of the beasts of the field, and the woman. Their exchange focused on what Adam and his mate were allowed to eat in the Garden.

The interchange contained both a direct lie and an accusation insinuating God's intention to unduly withhold a blessing from the couple. The subtle serpent's words were a direct challenge to God's authority and character, while Eve's response revealed her lack of accurate knowledge of God's directions to Adam.

Taking a close look at the initial discussions that occurred between the serpent and the woman, we find that the serpent begins in Genesis 3;

> *Now the serpent was more subtle than any beast of the field which the Lord God had made. And he said unto the woman, Yea, hath God said, Ye shall not eat of every tree of the garden?*

The woman's reply

> *And the woman said unto the serpent, We may eat of the fruit of the trees of the garden, But of the fruit of the tree which is in the midst of the garden, God hath said, Ye shall not eat of it, neither shall ye touch it, lest ye die.*

The serpent counter replied,

> *And the serpent said unto the woman, Ye shall not surely die: For God doth know that in the day ye eat thereof, then your eyes shall be opened, and ye shall be as gods, knowing good and evil. Genesis 3:1-5*

The serpent annulled the Lord God's instruction to the man.

First, the serpent insisted that death would not be their fate for disobeying the Lord God. When the serpent said, *"Ye shall not surely die,"* the woman believed the first lie spoken in opposition to God.

Next, the serpent implied that a great benefit would result from eating the prohibited fruit. The serpent implied that God was holding back the knowledge that they lacked, which would provide enhanced eyesight, making them like God.

The serpent deceived the woman into expecting a blessing of wisdom from the fruit, enabling the couple to discern between good and evil. The ultimate treachery promised that they would then be like God. Jesus spoke very clearly about the lying nature of the devil when He said,

> *Ye are of your father the devil, and the lusts of your father ye will do. He was a murderer from the beginning, and abode not in the truth, because there is no truth in him. When he speaketh a lie, he speaketh of his own: for he is a liar, and the father of it. John 8:44*

The woman's reaction (continuing in Genesis 3); *And when the woman saw that the tree was good for food, and that it was pleasant to the eyes, and a tree to be desired to make one wise, she took of the fruit thereof, and did eat, and gave also unto her husband with her; and he did eat.*

Immediate consequences resulted in major changes in the two humans;

> *And the eyes of them both were opened, and they knew that they were naked; and they sewed fig leaves together and made themselves aprons.*
>
> *And they heard the voice of the Lord God walking in the garden in the cool of the day: and Adam and his wife hid themselves from the presence of the Lord God amongst the trees of the garden. Genesis 3:6, 7, 8*

THE ENTRANCE OF SIN AND DEATH

The most damaging changes, however, were not immediately apparent. Paul, the apostle to the nations, revealed in his letter to the Romans the full extent of what the Lord God had warned Adam.

> *Wherefore, as by one man sin entered into the world, and death by sin; and so death passed upon all men, for that all have sinned: Romans 5:12*

Adam was formed by being directly molded from the soil of the earth. Eve was intricately fashioned from a part of him. But all other humans are generated and born into the world in the same universal manner. As they are born, all are dying sinners. There are no exceptions.

The curses applied to the two original humans were not only passed on to all their posterity, but all things in this creation suffer from Adam's disobedience. Consequently, the simple message of salvation by regeneration is generally held to be the proper remedy for this all-encompassing problem.

Ask most Christians, and you will likely receive their universal answer, which focuses on a conversation between Jesus and a Jewish Pharisee named Nicodemus.

> *There was a man of the Pharisees, named Nicodemus, a ruler of the Jews: The same came to Jesus by night, and said unto him, Rabbi, we know that thou art a teacher come from God: for no man can do these miracles that thou doest, except God be with him. Jesus answered and said unto him, Verily, verily, I say unto thee, Except a man be born again, he cannot see the kingdom of God. John 3:1-3*

Nicodemus began the conversation by referring to the miracles that Jesus performed. He also commended Jesus' teaching as coming from God. He confirmed that the miracles are proof that He has come from God, acknowledging that no general person can do such things unless God is present with him.

Jesus answered Nicodemus' initial statement by saying directly to him, *"except* (unless) *a man* (a certain one) *be born* (procreated, properly of the father, but by extension of the mother) *again* (from above, by analogy, from the first, by implication, anew), *he cannot see the Kingdom of God.*

This verse, likely the most well-known by modern Christians, is a summary of the common gospel, resulting in the benefit of salvation to those who believe it and confess it, to be born again.

When pressed for details, however, the body of truth expanding John's chapter three discussion with Nicodemus and the Lord will likely be limited in detail. Furthermore, individually examining the faith of a group of believers is likely to reveal a lack of harmony in their collective answers. It is reflective of the disunity arising out of the lack of detail.

An examination of the entire conversation between Jesus and Nicodemus may be helpful. The discussion continues:

> *Nicodemus saith unto him, how can a man be born when he is old? can he enter the second time into his mother's womb, and be born? John 3:4*

The man in verse four is not an individual human person, whether male or female. Nicodemus uses the generic term representing all humans, *anthropos*. His response is interesting in that, by using *anthropos*, he may be indicating that he was aware of the universal effect of the fallen condition of all humans.

> *Jesus answered, Verily, verily, I say unto thee, except a man be born of water and of the Spirit, he cannot enter into the kingdom of God. John 3:5*

Jesus' first response in verse three, *except a man be born again,* referred to the individual man, saying that he must be born again (genao anothen). In verse 5, Jesus adds the additional information, *"...of water and of the Spirit, he cannot enter into the kingdom of God."*

His response to Nicodemus, specifying that the remedy applies to individual persons, implies that each human must individually profit from the remedy.

Jesus continued;

> *That which is born of the flesh is flesh; and that which is born of the Spirit is spirit. Marvel not that I said unto thee, Ye must be born again. John 3:6-7*

It is of particular interest that the *"Ye"* in verse seven is not in the singular but is expressed as a plural. This indicates that all humans are in need of being born again, not just singular persons.

Contrasting flesh and spirit, Jesus speaks plainly to Nicodemus that whatever is born out of flesh is flesh, and whatever is born out of spirit is spirit. As to the first, the one being born of flesh is being generated out of flesh. The one being born of spirit is generated out of spirit. They originate from two separate and different ancestries.

Humans are generated out of Adam being brought into the world by human birth. Adam was the original man, out of whom all persons of the human race would find their human bodies originating in him. Adam was the original flesh, out of whom all persons of flesh have Adam as their biological source.

Both sin and death entered the world system, passing through Adam and all humans, both male and female, rendering each person a dying sinner.

Each human enters the world individually, without any involvement in their own birth. They cannot determine or choose their human parents.

As to everyone being born of spirit, are they born singularly, one at a time? Or were all born of the spirit at one time? This is an interesting, thought-provoking question.

Is the entire race of humanity born together at one time, and then each person gains the receipt of universal rebirth by faith? Was this about which Jesus challenged Nicodemus?

The narrative of John, Chapter 3, continues;

> *The wind bloweth where it listeth, and thou hearest the sound thereof, but canst not tell whence it cometh, and whither it goeth: so is every one that is born of the Spirit.*
>
> *Nicodemus answered and said unto him, How can these things be?*
>
> *Jesus answered and said unto him, Art thou a master of Israel, and knowest not these things?*
>
> *Verily, verily, I say unto thee, we speak that we do know, and testify that we have seen; and ye receive not our witness.*
>
> *If I have told you earthly things, and ye believe not, how shall ye believe, if I tell you of heavenly things? John 3:8-12*

Jesus reveals that the truth they are discussing in the night has a spiritual nature. Believers are meant to accept it. It is a matter of faith. Truth, which is saving truth, must be revealed by God's Spirit bearing witness with the saving words of the gospel.

However, the conversation continued without stopping at this point. Let us proceed then, hoping to gain the light of revelation that Nicodemus was being offered by the One Who is *the light of the world (John 8:12).*

> *And no man hath ascended up to heaven, but he that came down from heaven, even the Son of man which is in heaven.*
>
> *And as Moses lifted up the serpent in the wilderness, even so must the Son of man be lifted up:*
>
> *That whosoever believeth in him should not perish but have eternal life.*
>
> *For God so loved the world, that he gave his only begotten Son, that whosoever believeth in him should not perish, but have everlasting life.*
>
> *For God sent not his Son into the world to condemn the world; but that the world through him might be saved.*
>
> *He that believeth on him is not condemned: but he that believeth not is condemned already, because he hath not believed in the name of the only begotten Son of God.*
>
> *And this is the condemnation, that light is come into the world, and men loved darkness rather than light, because their deeds were evil.*
>
> *For every one that doeth evil hateth the light, neither cometh to the light, lest his deeds should be reproved.*
>
> *But he that doeth truth cometh to the light, that his deeds may be made manifest, that they are wrought in God. John 3:13-21*

Of particular note, when this momentous occasion is discussed between believers, they will claim "eternal life" as the ultimate benefit of their salvation. If questioned concerning this overwhelming grant, especially in relation to "eternal death," those professing this obvious gift will not receive any contradiction to the use of "eternal", which refers without question in their minds to last in perpetuity, without end. That is the likely common view.

So, it is essentially obvious to such believers that either a person has one or the other: eternal life or eternal death.

And, just as obvious to them, if you fall into the category of "eternal life" believers, you suppose that you are vastly blessed compared to those non-believers who are subject to "eternal death." It seems so painfully final.

As I have studied the scripture, using the tools of interpretation that are available to all who have access to the information bounty of the internet, I learned early on that the emphasis on the "eternal" was somewhat misapplied. I learned that "eternal" may actually apply to something that is limited in its application.

Let me explain. When you search the Greek of the New Testament, there is a word, *aionios,* which the King James interpreters rendered in the adjective form as "eternal." When, however, you look to the root of the word, you find the noun "aion." This word is clearly expressed as an era, or "eon," usually seen as a period of time of unspecified duration.

"Eternity," according to the view of "eternal death/eternal life" believers, is a period of time extending either into the past or into the future without a beginning or an end. But an "eon," the root word of *"aionios,"* appears to apply to a period of time with both a beginning and an end.

The unfortunate misapplication of this word when using it to describe an unlimited period of time is, I believe, one of the greatest errors that causes major disunity in the body of Christ. As a result, if divisions within the body are left unattended and uncorrected, it leads to significant loss and hurtful reproaches upon God.

Jesus came in the likeness of sinful flesh to tear down the walls of separation arising from unbelief, stubbornness, pride, and any cause of division. Paul expressed his belief that the members of the body of Christ are to love others as Jesus instructed and to secure *the unity of the faith (Ephesians 4:13)*.

The apostle Paul used the term *aionios*, 21 times. The King James translators consistently interpreted it as "eternal" or "everlasting." Fortunately, there are some more recent translations that have adjusted the word, *aionios*, often expressing it as *"age-lasting"*. One example is Young's translation, which reflects the limited duration of the word to which it is applied.

The importance of using "age-lasting" rather than "eternal" or "everlasting" cannot be overemphasized. When, for example, chastening is expressed as lasting forever, when, in fact, it is enduring for an age, the effect can hamper faith and cause a reproach upon God's name.

Paul described the wrath of God as the punishment upon those who do not obey God, rendering in the KJV in his second letter to the Thessalonians:

> *And to you who are troubled rest with us, when the Lord Jesus shall be revealed from heaven with his mighty angels,*
>
> *In flaming fire taking vengeance on them that know not God, and that obey not the gospel of our Lord Jesus Christ:*
>
> *Who shall be punished with everlasting destruction from the presence of the Lord, and from the glory of his power; II Thessalonians 1:7-9*

Does your faith agree with this length of duration? Is the separation from His face everlasting when scripture clearly teaches that every tongue shall confess and every knee shall bow before the Lord at the proper time? (Romans 14:11, Philippians 2:10)

The master deceiver has been at work since Adam and Eve were serving God in the Garden. The lies of the adversary continually abound. As Eve was deceived in the garden, the fraudster, as the father of all lies, has deceived innumerable truth seekers by saying that only certain people will live on in the afterlife, but far more will suffer eternal agony in the unquenchable fire.

An important step in the right direction would be to no longer speak of eternal or everlasting matters. Making such claims conflicts with God's word. The judgment of the eonian times is like the fire of God, which burns away the impurities of sin.

> *Who shall also confirm you unto the end, that ye may be blameless in the day of our Lord Jesus Christ. I Corinthians 1:7-8*

When the hosts of heaven and earth were created, there was an intimation that there would be great struggle involved in the godly process of bringing God's plan into reality. Humanity, when brought into the earth, would face a certain warfare, a fight of faith, so to speak.

When the Lord God spoke to Adam, Eve, and the serpent after the fall occurred, a certain word and expression was spoken by God that characterized the imminent conflict.

> *And I will put enmity between thee and the woman, and between thy seed and her seed; it shall bruise thy head, and thou shalt bruise his heel. Genesis 3:15*

What God created, His adversary sought immediately to destroy and rule.

But there is a promise in the verse that, through *her seed,* God would gain a victory, a reversal of the *fall*. Let us together understand, believe, and proclaim that victory, which will be accomplished through *her seed,* the Lord Jesus Christ, God's only begotten Son.

We are to believe that all things are possible with God.

God's divine plan will not fail.

CHAPTER 2

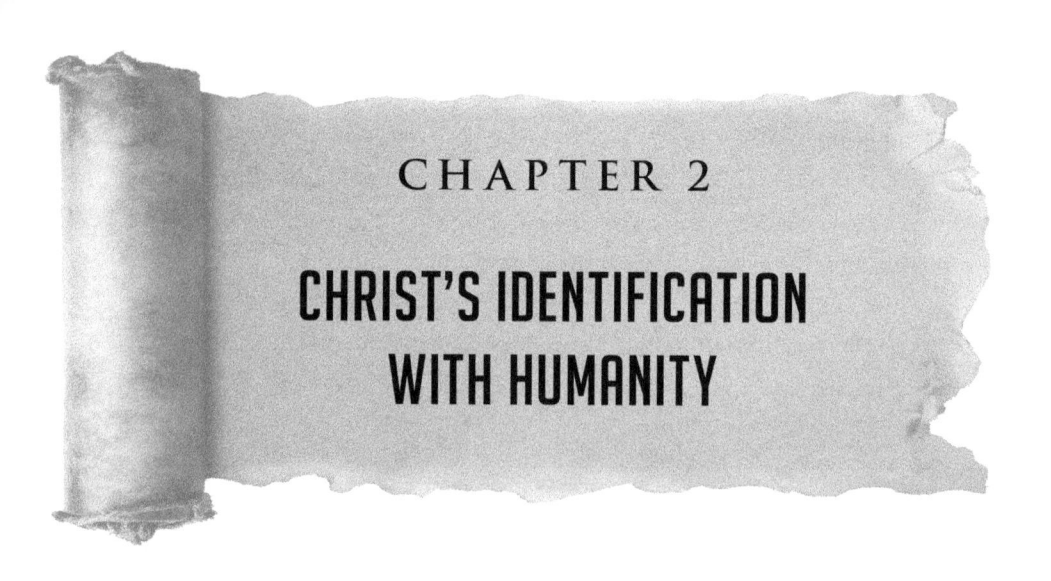

CHRIST'S IDENTIFICATION WITH HUMANITY

THE DUAL ROLES OF JESUS
THE SON OF GOD AND THE SON OF MAN

Through Jesus, the first creation came into existence.

In the beginning was the Word, and the Word was with God, and the Word was God. The same was in the beginning with God. All things were made by him; and without him was not anything made that was made. In him was life; and the life was the light of men. John 1:1-4

Paul also said in Ephesians:

And to make all men see what the fellowship of the mystery is, which from the beginning of the world hath been hid in God, who created all things by Jesus Christ. Ephesians 3:9

In the beginning of the first creation, Jesus is described by John as the Word, the *Logos* of God.

The first creation came into existence through Him.

In the first creation, Adam was the beginning of humanity on earth. He was the first man brought into the world, as chronicled in Genesis, chapters 1 and 2. The entire race of humanity came out of Adam. His wife, Eve, was the first human to be taken out of him..

Christ, as the first of all things, is contrasted with Adam, the first of all humans.

As the first human, Adam represented all of those who came out of him. He was the pattern, the prototype. He was the first of a race, the first of those who would come into existence in God's likeness.

The first creation, as described in Genesis, was marred and upended by Adam's defection, as he was enticed by his mate to believe the lie of the serpent in the garden. In Adam, therefore, all humans are subject to the enemies of God, sin and death.

Adam is the head of the *Old Humanity in the Old Creation.*

In Jesus, the new creation is presently coming into existence. When the new creation is fully realized, the old creation will be set aside.

> *Therefore, if any man be in Christ, he is a new creature: old things are passed away; behold, all things are made new. II Corinthians 5:17*

All of humanity was in Adam when God formed him in the garden. And, as we will subsequently discover, all of the new humanity comes out of Christ and into the new creation.

Consequently, what Adam experienced in the Garden when he disobeyed the Lord God affected all humans. He was the head of the human race. As a result, each family member, both male and female, inherited his fallen condition as they entered the world through their generations.

The debilitating experience of both sin and death is common to all humans, being transmitted from the original man and passing through to all without exception.

The apostle Paul summarizes Adam's offense toward the Lord God in his letter to the Romans, in chapter 5, as it affected all humans.

> *Wherefore, as by one man sin entered into the world, and death by sin; and so death passed upon all men, for that all have sinned. (For until the law, sin was in the world, but sin is not imputed when there is no law. Nevertheless, death reigned from Adam to Moses, even over them that had not sinned after the similitude of Adam's transgression, who is the figure of him that was to come. Romans 5:12-14*

Adam, as a type of Christ, an example or pattern, is the first person to be a prefigure of the One who was to come. In the first man, Adam, all humans find their pattern in him. As he is from the earth, every person deriving their humanity from Adam is also earthy when brought into the world. All human bodies are made from the soil, the original source of material that formed Adam's body.

In the second man, the pattern holds true in Christ, as all humans in the new creation are patterned after the Lord Jesus Christ.

> *The first man is of the earth, earthy; the second man is the Lord from heaven. I Corinthians 15:47*

The Lord God enlightened Adam as to the consequences of eating the fruit of the tree of the knowledge of good and evil. Immediately upon ingesting the fruit, Adam became a dying sinner. Similarly, Eve suffered the same fate as Adam when he ate the forbidden fruit, as she was taken out of him. She also became a dying sinner. What Adam experienced affected all who would follow. All humans totally identify with Adam in these matters.

The original couple, man and wife, were forced out of the garden, forfeiting their fellowship with God, their divine creator. Paul, the apostle to the nations, describes in his letter to the Ephesians the fallen condition that all of their posterity would share.

> *That at that time ye were without Christ, being aliens from the commonwealth of Israel, and strangers from the covenants of promise, having no hope, and without God in the world. Ephesians 2:12*

The state of mortality has dominated mankind in a universal manner until God, the Father, instituted a remedy through His only begotten Son. The Son of God, having His abode with His Father in the heavenly realm, willingly emptied Himself and came to earth to rescue humanity. His saving work to rescue Adam's family is to reunite humanity with their creator and restore fellowship, as they were created in the image of God.

Paul describes the Son of God's glorious, humbling descent into the human realm in his letter to the Philippians.

> *Let this mind be in you, which was also in Christ Jesus: Who, being in the form of God, thought it not robbery to be equal with God: But made himself of no reputation, and took upon him the form of a servant, and was made in the likeness of men: And being found in fashion as a man, he humbled himself, and became obedient unto death, even the death of the cross.*
>
> *Wherefore God also hath highly exalted him, and given him a name which is above every name: That at the name of Jesus every knee should bow, of things in heaven, and things in earth, and things under the earth; And that every tongue should confess that Jesus Christ is Lord, to the glory of God the Father. Philippians 2:5-11*

Jesus Christ, as the Son of God, willingly relinquished His divine glory so that His Father, through the power of the Holy Spirit, could conceive Him as the Son of man in the sacred act of being born to a human mother.

Jesus, in His role on earth, became the kinsman redeemer for the entire race that finds its human source in Adam. Being unable to redeem themselves, they find a new source of life in Christ's resurrection.

Mary, His human mother, conceived the Holy One without being married to a human male. In that sacred-generated state, Jesus was not dying, nor was He influenced or controlled by sin, as were all other humans born of a human father as direct descendants of Adam.

Jesus was the only begotten of the Father, as the Holy Spirit of God overshadowed Mary, his human mother, through what is described as the Virgin Birth. The child within her shared with all other humans the complete meaning of being a human child of God, with the exception of sin and death. He was brought forth in the likeness of sinful flesh.

Having no human biological father, Jesus was not subject to mortality, nor was he born a sinner. He was without sin. He was also not dying when He was born, as is true of all offspring of Adam, as it is written, *"For as in Adam all die."(I Corinthians 15:22a)*

Jesus became one of us. He was destined to completely identify with us all.

Jesus was in God, and God was in him. Jesus was in the world, but not of the world. He entered the world to summon all those chosen to be united with Him, enabling the world to believe that the Father had sent Him to fulfill His unique mission.

Humanity, now separated from God and from Christ by Adam's transgression, must be recreated. Christ and God together will reunite humanity. The Old Humanity was not to be repaired or restored back to Adam's original state, but retired once and for all.

First, Christ was joined to the Old Humanity so that He could identify with Adam's posterity. Then, when crucified and entering death, the Old Humanity was placed in the tomb, in Jesus, as the last Adam (I

Corinthians 15:45-47). The New Humanity was created in Him, the second man, when Jesus was brought back to life.

Adam was the first man on earth to be made a living soul. Jesus Christ is the second man, the Lord from heaven, a life-giving spirit (I Corinthians 15:45).

The Son of God emptied Himself and became the Son of man in the *likeness of men*, regenerating humanity through the Father's creation of a New Humanity in Him. Adam was originally made in the likeness of God. The New Humanity would now conform to the image of Christ, who is the image of God.

Outwardly, Jesus was in the likeness of sinful flesh. By the same spiritual principle that all of humanity was in Adam in the Garden, all of humanity was in Christ as the Son of man, as the last Adam.

He, as the Son of man, was the fulness of the Godhead in bodily form (Colossians 2:9). He put an end to the fallen image of mankind, marred and disfigured by sin and death.

Jesus as the Son of God is testified to many times in the New Testament scriptures by multiple witnesses. He did not insist on calling attention to the title of God's Son directly but was declared to be the Son of God upon His resurrection, as Paul said in the letter to the Romans.

> *Paul, a servant of Jesus Christ, called to be an apostle, separated unto the gospel of God, (Which he had promised afore by his prophets in the holy scriptures,) Concerning his Son Jesus Christ our Lord, which was made of the seed of David according to the flesh; And declared to be the Son of God with power, according to the spirit of holiness, by the resurrection from the dead: Romans 1:1-4*

On numerous occasions, as recorded in the gospel narratives of Matthew, Mark, Luke, and John, the title Son of God, was proclaimed by others, especially by unclean spirits that recognized Him. They made reference to His future judgment of them, insisting that His presence was premature during His ministry on earth. (See Mark 3:11, Mark 5:7, Luke 8:28.)

The most direct challenge to the Lord as to His high station as God's Son came from the tempter in the wilderness. Matthew gives the account:

> *And when the tempter came to him, he said, If thou be the Son of God, command that these stones be made bread. But he answered and said, It is written, Man shall not live by bread alone, but by every word that proceedeth out of the mouth of God. Then the devil taketh him up into the holy city, and setteth him on a pinnacle of the temple, And saith unto him, If thou be the Son of God, cast thyself down: for it is written, He shall give his angels charge concerning thee: and in their hands they shall bear thee up, lest at any time thou dash thy foot against a stone. Matthew 4:3-6*

It is apparent that the tempter sought to lure him to demonstrate his sonship of God. But Jesus focused on His role as the Son of man. In the final sections of Matthew's account, Jesus is brought before the chief priests, elders, and all the council seeking false witnesses against Him, so as to put Him to death. Many false witnesses came to testify, with the final two gaining the ire of the High Priest concerning the destruction of the temple of God. He had spoken of His body being raised again after three days, but the two false witnesses said it was concerning the actual temple, not the temple of His body. He did not answer their accusations.

> *And the high priest arose, and said unto him, Answerest thou nothing? what is it which these witness against thee? But Jesus held his peace, And the high priest answered and said unto him, I adjure thee by the living God, that thou tell us whether thou be the Christ, the Son of God. Jesus saith unto him, Thou hast said: nevertheless I say unto you, Hereafter shall ye see the Son of man sitting on the right hand of power, and coming in the clouds of heaven. Matthew 26:62-64*

Jesus did not provide an affirmative answer concerning being the Christ, the Son of God, but said, *"Thou hast said."* The final words of His reply affirmed His preferred title as to the role of the Son of Man, describing that they would see Him sitting at God's right hand and then coming in the clouds of heaven.

In the Old Testament, the title phrase, Son of Man, was used extensively in Ezekiel's prophecy, over 90 verses. The Lord God used the phrase to identify Ezekiel's role as the watchman over Israel.

Daniel, the prophet, was also referred to as the Son of Man, receiving from the Lord God a vision of world-wide kingdoms culminating in the vision of the final kingdom, which described the Son of Man coming to earth from heaven.

> *I saw in the night visions, and, behold, one like the Son of man came with the clouds of heaven, and came to the Ancient of days, and they brought him near before him. Daniel 7:13*

The reference that Daniel, as well as Ezekiel, was also called the Son of Man is found in Daniel 8:17.

> *So he came near where I stood: and when he came, I was afraid, and fell upon my face: but he said unto me, Understand, O son of man: for at the time of the end shall be the vision. Daniel 8:17*

Mark, in his New Testament gospel, reports that the centurion, who was among the company that attended the crucifixion, saw the earthquake shaking the ground beneath them and, fearing greatly, exclaimed, *"Truly, this was the Son of God"* (Mark 15:39).

One of the few times that the dual roles of Jesus were cited occurred in Peter's revelation in Matthew 16. In Peter's testimony, he described Jesus as *"the Christ, the Son of the living God."* This was in response to the question the Lord had posed to His disciples.

The question from Jesus was to hear from the disciples what the people were saying as to His identity. None of their responses were accurate. When He asked the disciples, *"Who do they say that I, the Son of man, am?* They gave different answers, ranging from the prophet Elijah to John the Baptist or others, but no one made the connection that Peter was revealed (Matthew 16:13–19). Paul, the apostle to the nations, would fully unveil the mystery of Christ in his letters, connecting it to the revelation given to Peter.

The revelation rock upon which Christ's church would be built was that Jesus, the Son of living God, was also the Christ, the Son of Man. Jesus declared that flesh and blood did not disclose this to Peter, but rather it was revealed to him through a spiritual revelation from the Father in heaven.

One of the chief obstacles facing the fallen race of Adam is to attest that Jesus is the Son of the living God. One of the major obstacles to believers In Jesus is seeing and understanding that Jesus Christ, as the Son of God, is also the Son of Man.

His role as the Son of Man is the central truth of the gospel presented by Paul. This vital truth is a complement to the truth that Jesus has been, is, and will always be the Son of God. Paul's letters, as we shall see, magnify these connected roles to bring to the surface His fulness as God's complement. God the Father's overwhelming love is displayed in the person of Christ, His Son, and our blessed Redeemer and Lord.

In His divine role as God's Son, Jesus, as the Word of God, completed the first creation that was marred by the disobedience of the first man, Adam. In His assumed role as the Son of Man, He divested Himself of His divine glory so as to identify completely with the fallen race that was originally created in God's image.

To be totally identified with Adam's posterity, Jesus took upon Himself the form of a human, being in the likeness of sinful flesh. His virgin birth was by the generation of God, His Father, placing Him in His earthly mother, Mary. Joseph, recognized as His earthly father, was not the biological parent. Therefore, when he was born, Jesus was free from sin and death.

Without sin and not subject to death, he had to experience both of these enemies of God so that he could identify with humanity in a complete capacity.

Prior to His arrest, trial, and horrendous bodily punishment, the process of His identification was limited to experiencing the gamut of human emotions that affect all people. Even to the point of weeping, He felt the common sentiments, passion, and sensory inputs during his exchanges with others.

Jesus felt both rejection and abandonment. His overwhelming feelings of being alone often sent Him to places of solitude, allowing Him to rejoin with His Heavenly Father in prayerful communication between them.

But to be fully joined to His human family, Jesus had to be made subject to sin and then die. Death began to overtake Him as His precious blood began to flow out of His body during His sorrows, as foretold by Isaiah.

> *Surely he hath borne our griefs, and carried our sorrows: yet we did esteem him stricken, smitten of God, and afflicted.*
>
> *But he was wounded for our transgressions, he was bruised for our iniquities: the chastisement of our peace was upon him; and with his stripes we are healed. Isaiah 53:4-5*

The Lamb of God was ordained to experience the dying process faced by every human from the moment of birth in a mortal human body. John the

Baptist was the first to testify of His fateful sacrifice when he placed Him into the water at the Jordan River.

> *These things were done in Bethabara, beyond Jordan, where John was baptizing.*
>
> *The next day John seeth Jesus coming unto him and saith, Behold the Lamb of God, which taketh away the sin of the world. John 1:28-29*

The judgment of the priests, elders of the people, and the general crowd of faithless evildoers pressed the Romans into exacting the sentence of the cross, where death would completely overtake Him.

Not only was Jesus to experience dying and death, but the Lord of Glory had to be joined to sin itself. How could His Father consent to such unspeakable events? Paul, the apostle to the Gentiles, was the first to receive this divine mystery. He reported God's answer in his second letter to the church at Corinth.

> *Now then we are ambassadors for Christ, as though God did beseech you by us: we pray you in Christ's stead, be ye reconciled to God.*
>
> *For he hath made him to be sin for us, who knew no sin; that we might be made the righteousness of God in him. I Corinthians 5:20-21*

The exchange of sin for Him followed by righteousness for us is the reason for the Father's choice to have His only begotten Son subjected to both sin and death.

Jesus, when He came in the likeness of sin's flesh, identified fully with us as individual members of the Old Humanity. He experienced both the pain and joy of being human. Jesus experienced all the sufferings of mankind. He was rejected. He was misunderstood. He was mocked and reproached during His ministry. All of which led to His final days in the city of His Father's house, Jerusalem, the holy city of peace.

Jesus, as the Son of Man, sought to live a simple, humble life. We first learned of His modest and unpretentious state when He answered the scribe, who said unto Him, *"Master, I will follow thee withersoever thou goest."* (Matthew 8:19b).

> *And Jesus saith unto him, the foxes have holes, and the birds of the air have nests; but the Son of man hath not where to lay his head.*
> *Matthew 8:20*

In His simplistic state, however, the Son of Man was given great authority.

A man, sick of the palsy lying on his bed, was brought to Jesus, when he exposed the blasphemous accusations of the scribes as He ministered to the sick man.

> *And he entered into a ship, and passed over, and came into his own city.*
>
> *And, behold, they brought to him a man sick of the palsy, lying on a bed: and Jesus seeing their faith said unto the sick of the palsy; Son, be of good cheer; thy sins be forgiven thee.*
>
> *And, behold, certain of the scribes said within themselves, This man blasphemeth.*
>
> *And Jesus knowing their thoughts said, Wherefore think ye evil in your hearts?*
>
> *For whether is easier, to say, Thy sins be forgiven thee; or to say, Arise, and walk?*

> *But that ye may know that the Son of man hath power on earth to forgive sins, (then saith he to the sick of the palsy,) Arise, take up thy bed, and go unto thine house.*
>
> *And he arose and departed for his house. Matthew 9:1-7*

His compassion and mercy toward the afflicted were the hallmarks of His ministry as the Son of Man. He wanted the accusing scribes to know that the delegated influence of His authority extended both to the healing of the sicknesses of humanity and to the wondrous right to forgive sins.

Further on, in Matthew's gospel, Jesus provoked the ire of the religious Spirit of the legalistic Pharisees concerning His actions on the Sabbath day.

> *At that time Jesus went on the sabbath day through the corn; and his disciples were an hungered, and began to pluck the ears of corn and to eat.*
>
> *But when the Pharisees saw it, they said unto him, Behold, thy disciples do that which is not lawful to do upon the sabbath day.*
>
> *But he said unto them, Have ye not read what David did, when he was an hungered, and they that were with him;*
>
> *How he entered into the house of God, and did eat the shewbread, which was not lawful for him to eat, neither for them which were with him, but only for the priests?*
>
> *Or have ye not read in the law, how that on the sabbath days the priests in the temple profane the sabbath, and are blameless?*
>
> *But I say unto you, That in this place is one greater than the temple.*

But if ye had known what this meaneth, I will have mercy, and not sacrifice, ye would not have condemned the guiltless.

For the Son of man is Lord even of the sabbath day. Matthew 12:1-8

There is a volume of wisdom and insight in this encounter between Jesus, the Son of Man, and the Pharisees. They were legalists. He was full of mercy and truth, as John had described Him in his gospel.

And the Word was made flesh, and dwelt among us, (and we beheld his glory, the glory as of the only begotten of the Father,) full of grace and truth. John 1:14

Jesus demonstrates to the elite class of the Hebrews how Adam's disobedience caused the forfeiture and loss of the true ministry of man. Jesus, not only demonstrating the obedience of faith in His ministry, but He also spoke of those things, yet in the future, which He as the Son of man would accomplish. He spoke of things pertaining to Him that the people of Israel would understand, especially when He referred to things of the past to link with things that He, as the Son of man, would experience.

When certain of the scribes and Pharisees sought to provoke Jesus into showing them a sign, Jesus characterized them as an evil and adulterous generation. They were, so I believe, mocking Him to perform a miraculous sign, which would prove Him to be the Son of God, and if He did not show forth that power, it would prove to them that He was an imposter.

But He came forth, not to prove that He was God's Son but to demonstrate His identity with all of humanity as the Son of man. This was His unique mission.

Then certain of the scribes and of the Pharisees answered, saying, Master, we would see a sign from thee.

> *But he answered and said unto them, An evil and adulterous generation seeketh after a sign; and there shall no sign be given to it, but the sign of the prophet Jonas:*
>
> *For as Jonas was three days and three nights in the whale's belly; so shall the Son of man be three days and three nights in the heart of the earth.*
>
> *The men of Nineveh shall rise in judgment with this generation and shall condemn it: because they repented at the preaching of Jonas; and, behold, a greater than Jonas is here.*
>
> *The queen of the south shall rise up in the judgment with this generation and shall condemn it: for she came from the uttermost parts of the earth to hear the wisdom of Solomon; and, behold, a greater than Solomon is here. Matthew 12:38-42*

They demanded a miraculous sign in the same manner as the adversary in the wilderness tempted Him. If the temptation to prove His power over the elements overcame Him, He would follow in Adam's steps of departure from the Father's will, and His mission would fail.

Using a portion of Israel's holy writings, Jesus foretold that as the Son of man, like Jonah spending time in the belly of the fish, He would be placed in burial in the heart of the earth. This was one of many fateful sayings about Jesus' mission as the Son of Man to experience through His sacrificial suffering and death.

Jesus also explained that the Son of Man was in the world to sow the seeds of the gospel. He used the commonly understood process of the sower casting seed into the earth in view of an appropriate harvest to follow.

> *Another parable put he forth unto them, saying, The kingdom of heaven is like to a grain of mustard seed, which a man took, and sowed in his field:*

> *Which indeed is the least of all seeds: but when it is grown, it is the greatest among herbs, and becometh a tree, so that the birds of the air come and lodge in the branches thereof.*
>
> *Another parable spake he unto them; The kingdom of heaven is like unto leaven, which a woman took, and hid in three measures of meal, till the whole was leavened.*
>
> *All these things spake Jesus unto the multitude in parables; and without a parable spake he not unto them:*
>
> *That it might be fulfilled which was spoken by the prophet, saying, I will open my mouth in parables; I will utter things which have been kept secret from the foundation of the world.*
>
> *Then Jesus sent the multitude away and went into the house: and his disciples came unto him, saying, Declare unto us the parable of the tares of the field.*
>
> *He answered and said unto them, He that soweth the good seed is the Son of man;*
>
> *The field is the world; the good seed are the children of the kingdom; but the tares are the children of the wicked one; Matthew 13:31-38*

This parable described that the Son of Man would be sowing the gospel into the world as compared to a human sower of seed casting the seed of his crops into the ground. Jesus referred to the harvest as the sowing of the *children of the kingdom*, who would be sown into the world as good seed.

These children, as described here, are not limited to the younger members of the household. The word is *huios* (Strong's #G5207, "son," denoting kinship, generally used of the offspring of men).

1. Doctor Strong, in his widely familiar Concordance, expanded the term *son*, *"huios,"* as follows in subsection 3., describing Christ as the Son of man. Dr. Strong described *huios* as a term. "describing man, carrying the connotation of weakness and mortality
2. symbolically denotes the fifth kingdom in Daniel 7:13, and by this term, its humanity is indicated in contrast with the barbarity and ferocity of the four preceding kingdoms, typified by the four beasts.
3. Used by Christ himself, doubtless in order that he might intimate his Messiahship and also that he might designate himself as the head of the human family, the man, the one who both furnished the pattern of the perfect man and acted on behalf of all mankind. Christ seems to have preferred this to other Messianic titles because, by its lowliness, it was least suited to foster the expectation of an earthly Messiah in royal splendor."

Jesus, as the Son of Man, experienced the gamut of human emotions up to Calvary's cross. As His suffering began in the garden, His fervent prayer to the Father produced sweat like drops of blood.

He was arrested and led away, knowing that the cup of the Father's judgment upon Adam's family was His to drink to the fullest. Then, receiving the painful scourging that followed His mock trial, His identification with humanity came closer yet to its fulfillment.

What He lacked in the process of complete identification was the ability to confront and defeat the two enemies that entered the creation through Adam—both sin and death. The Father allowed Him to taste sin for us, as God cursed Him for being hanged on the tree, as it is written;

> *And if a man have committed a sin worthy of death, and he be to be put to death, and thou hang him on a tree:*

> *His body shall not remain all night upon the tree, but thou shalt in any wise bury him that day; (for he that is hanged is accursed of God;) that thy land be not defiled, which the Lord thy God giveth thee for an inheritance. Deuteronomy 21:22-23*

His death soon followed. When He gave up His spirit to the Father, He said, *"It is finished."* His identification with the human race was complete.

To every believer who may read these words, it is vital that you understand and believe that Jesus totally became united with humanity, as He identified completely with all the human race. In that capacity, He was able to bear the burden, not only of each individual's sins but of sin itself.

As a final judgment for Adam's disobedience, Jesus died. The penalty of sin is death. He tasted death for all of humanity. The death of God's Son, as the Son of Man, ended the humanity that came through Adam.

His next appearance as the Son of Man will be manifested at His return.

> *The Son of man shall send forth his angels, and they shall gather out of his kingdom all things that offend, and them which do iniquity; Matthew 13:41*

Then, as the Son of Man, Jesus will execute judgment, as John reports in his gospel.

> *For as the Father hath life in himself; so hath he given to the Son to have life in himself;*
>
> *And hath given him authority to execute judgment also, because he is the Son of man.*

> *Marvel not at this: for the hour is coming, in the which all that are in the graves shall hear his voice,*
>
> *And shall come forth; they that have done good, unto the resurrection of life; and they that have done evil, unto the resurrection of damnation. John 5:26-29*

All of humanity will be raised from death. Death will come to an end.

> *I can of mine own self do nothing: as I hear, I judge: and my judgment is just; because I seek not mine own will, but the will of the Father which hath sent me. John 5:30*

He knows exactly what we go through as humans in this fallen world because He went through the same in His life, through His sufferings, and finally in His death.

Read again Romans 5:8-21 to see God's salvation in Christ as contrasted to Adam's cause of sin and death's entrance.

> *But God commendeth his love toward us, in that, while we were yet sinners, Christ died for us.*
>
> *Much more then, being now justified by his blood, we shall be saved from wrath through him.*
>
> *For if, when we were enemies, we were reconciled to God by the death of his Son, much more, being reconciled, we shall be saved by his life.*
>
> *And not only so, but we also joy in God through our Lord Jesus Christ, by whom we have now received the atonement.*

Wherefore, as by one man sin entered into the world, and death by sin; and so death passed upon all men, for that all have sinned:

(For until the law sin was in the world: but sin is not imputed when there is no law.

Nevertheless, death reigned from Adam to Moses, even over them that had not sinned after the similitude of Adam's transgression, who is the figure of him that was to come.

But not as the offence, so also is the free gift. For if through the offence of one many be dead, much more the grace of God, and the gift by grace, which is by one man, Jesus Christ, hath abounded unto many.

And not as it was by one that sinned, so is the gift: for the judgment was by one to condemnation, but the free gift is of many offences unto justification.

For if by one man's offence death reigned by one; much more they which receive abundance of grace and of the gift of righteousness shall reign in life by one, Jesus Christ.)

Therefore, as by the offence of one judgment came upon all men to condemnation; even so by the righteousness of one the free gift came upon all men unto justification of life.

For as by one man's disobedience many were made sinners, so by the obedience of one shall many be made righteous.

Moreover, the law entered, that the offence might abound. But where sin abounded, grace did much more abound:

That as sin hath reigned unto death, even so might grace reign through righteousness unto eternal life by Jesus Christ our Lord.

Here is Paul's summary of the common salvation for all that are called in this era of grace. This is the essence of Paul's salvation message, his gospel.

> *Moreover, brethren, I declare unto you the gospel which I preached unto you, which also ye have received, and wherein ye stand;*
>
> *By which also ye are saved, if ye keep in memory what I preached unto you, unless ye have believed in vain.*
>
> *For I delivered unto you first of all that which I also received, how that Christ died for our sins according to the scriptures;*
>
> *And that he was buried, and that he rose again the third day according to the scriptures: I Corinthians 15:1-4*

This is the common gospel, the message that is common to all those who, in this era of reigning grace, are called to God. They are those who have been determined beforehand to receive a calling from God in this present time.

Finally, they are to believe that He died for their sins. His blood justifies them for the forgiveness of their sins. They are to believe that He was buried. They took Him down from the cross and placed Him within the tomb. They are to believe that He rose again. He is the first fruit of the resurrection.

These scriptural truths describe the common faith of all who are believers, members of Christ's body.

A significant goal of this manuscript is to differentiate between saving truth that is common to all believers by means of Christ's blood and joint truth that brings unity between believers by means of Christ's body, both by His death and His resurrection.

Understanding the dual roles of Jesus will shed light on these vital matters.

CHAPTER 3

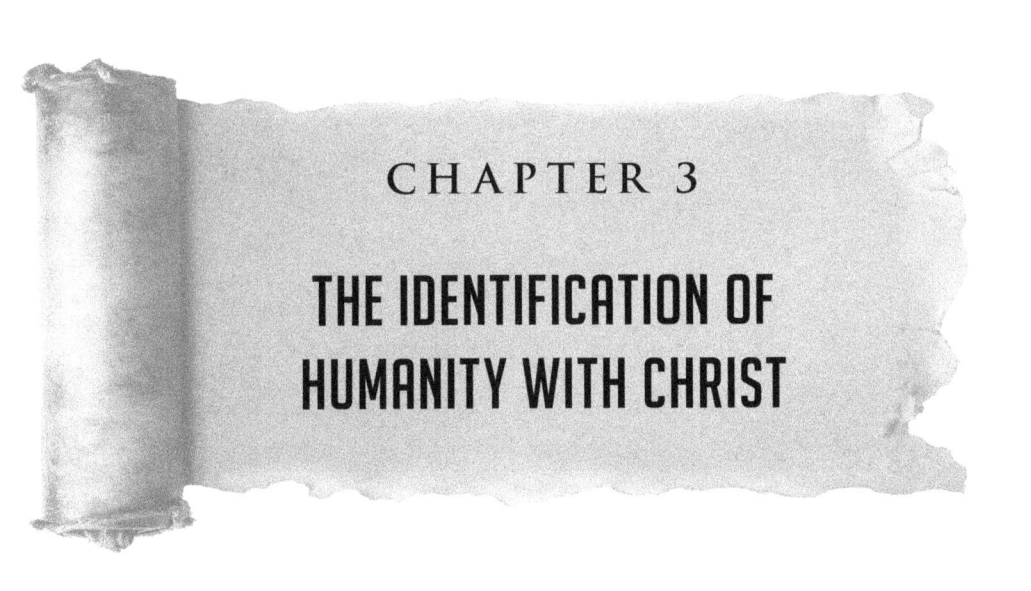

THE IDENTIFICATION OF HUMANITY WITH CHRIST

BECOMING SONS OF GOD IN HIM

Jesus fully identified with humanity as the Son of Man. In doing so, He became the last Adam (I Corinthians 15:45). He finished the work His Father sent Him to complete at His first coming.

As the suffering servant, He reclaimed humanity while overthrowing the works of the adversary as the Son of God (1 John 3:8).

He is also the second man (I Corinthians 15:47). He began a new work that His Father sent Him to commence with His resurrection from the dead.

> *And so it is written: The first man Adam was made a living soul; the last Adam was made a quickening spirit.*
>
> *Howbeit that was not first which is spiritual, but that which is natural; and afterward that which is spiritual.*
>
> *The first man is of the earth, earthy; the second man is the Lord from heaven.*

> *As is the earthy, such are they also that are earthy: and as is the heavenly, such are they also that are heavenly.*
>
> *And as we have borne the image of the earthy, we shall also bear the image of the heavenly.*
>
> *Now this I say, brethren, that flesh and blood cannot inherit the kingdom of God; neither doth corruption inherit incorruption. I Corinthians 45-50*

Jesus came to separate the *Old* from the *New,* to end the *Old* and *begin the New.*

During His ministry on earth, He was born into the nation of Israel to minister to His people. He spoke to His people many times, comparing the old with the new. These parables speak to us today as well.

> *No man putteth a piece of new cloth unto an old garment, for that which is put in to fill it up taketh from the garment, and the rent is made worse. Matthew 9:16*

Jesus repeated this parable in Mark 2:21 and Luke 5:36. Jesus taught that while there is a place for the old, the new is not intended to restore it. If we try to combine the two, the result will be detrimental to both.

> *Neither do men put new wine into old bottles: else the bottles break, and the wine runneth out, and the bottles perish: but they put new wine into new bottles, and both are preserved. Matthew 9:17*

Likewise, these sayings were repeated in Mark 22 and Luke 5:37.

Jesus said that the new cannot be joined with the old. It will not produce an acceptable hybrid of the two.

Now, in this era of grace, believers are to fully identify with Him as He identified with us.

As we have stated before, Jesus, as the Son of man, fully identified with all of humanity. We may mistakenly conclude that He came for only those who heeded His call, but the inclusive and complete truth is that He came for all of humanity to end the Old and begin and complete the New.

Those who embrace the truths of Paul's gospel in this time of reigning grace will be counted as members of Christ's body, the church, during this present time of his gospel's authority. All others will see the truth later.

Believers become members of His body as the blood of Christ covers their sins, saving that person from the wrath of God (Romans 5:8). Every believer becomes a child of God and a member of God's family.

As children, their heavenly Father does not want them to remain minors. He wants to advance their faith through His truth to gain the position of mature members of the family. Believers are to become *sons* of God.

A son fulfills a role of leadership and authority in the family of God.

The Father's method is to advance all believers from being *common* children of His family to reaching the majority, a state of established and developed participation in the Father's household. In this sought-after state, the sons of the family will practice together noble positions of authority and respectability not possible in the initial stages of faith. In the course of time, the Father places His sons in roles as joint heirs with Christ.

And now, we are to *press toward the prize of the high calling of God in Christ Jesus (Philippians 3:14)*, becoming fully identified with Him.

We are to know and proclaim that His saving work encompasses all that the Father asked of Him—to finish the Old and to initiate the New.

We are to apprehend His saving work as the Son of man. We know that He is the Son of God, capable of all manner of unlimited wondrous works.

Jesus came to earth from heaven to bring humanity back into unity with God. He came to end the separation of the "Old Humanity," by means of His death on the cross and to have created in Himself the "New Humanity" whereby the unity between God and man is restored in Christ.

The unity of sons joined to Christ is permanent, as Paul proclaims. There can be no separation.

> *Who shall separate us from the love of Christ? Shall trouble or hardship or persecution or famine or nakedness or danger or sword? As it is written:*
>
> *"For your sake we face death all day long; we are considered as sheep to be slaughtered".*
>
> *No, in all these things we are more than conquerors through him who loved us. For I am convinced that neither death nor life, neither angels nor demons, neither the present nor the future, nor any powers, neither height nor depth, nor anything else in all creation, will be able to separate us from the love of God that is in Christ Jesus our Lord. Romans 8:35-39*

As we become fully convinced that Jesus joined Himself entirely with us, we must also become fully convinced that we are joined completely with Him.

In our role as the heirs of God, we are to be confident that we can share in all that Jesus is to God. We are His body, the fulness of God in Him (Ephesians 1:23).

> *And to know the love of Christ, which passeth knowledge, that ye might be filled with all the fulness of God. Ephesians 3:19*

Understanding the saving truths of the Lord's accomplishments is a spiritual matter that requires that we "see" with new eyes, the eyes of our understanding (Ephesians 1:17). It is not enough to know an abundance of what the scripture says, but to know what it means in such clarity that we can relate to others what they also need to envision.

Spiritual vision requires an *"apokalupsis" (Strong's #G602, a noun meaning a laying bear, a disclosure of truth)*. It comes from a verb, *"apokalupto" (Strong's #601, to uncover what has been veiled, to make known, to disclose)*.

The unveiling of spiritual truth is the work of the Holy Spirit, the spirit of truth, sent forth on the Day of Pentecost to magnify the truths concerning Christ, the truths that will renew the mind (Romans 12:2). The poured-out Spirit is now the indwelling Spirit, uniting our spirit with His Spirit. Jesus is dwelling within all believers through the indwelling Spirit of God (Romans 8:9, 10).

When Jesus inquired of His disciples in Matthew 16 concerning His identity, the question He posed to them was intended to unveil their view and understanding of His uniqueness. If they were not informed in a proper manner, they would then to know exactly their deficiency and then receive the adjusting truth that would bring them back to their proper place and faith.

We learned in our previous discussion that Jesus actually had two distinct roles. He is and will always be the Son of God, being part of the Godhead, the fulness of God dwelling in Him (Colossians 1:19), along with His Father and the Spirit of Holiness. He is both the Son of God and the Son of man.

We, as Adam's race, are all considered the "Old Humanity" (*palios anthropos*). In our old state brought about by Adam's fall, we are faced with two major problems acquired at our birth as generations come forth out of Adam. We are all dying as the spirit life of God keeps us sustained but is ebbing away.

Also, because we do not have within us the power of God, we are subject to sin, doing things we know are not proper, things that dishonor God and do not glorify God. We are all dying sinners.

The sins that we commit, whether knowing what we do or not knowing but sinning just the same, must be dealt with through judgment that comes from God. People commonly refer to such judgment as His wrath.

He contrasts His anger towards sin with His mercy and forgiveness towards the sinner. His divine mercy is displayed in the sacrifice of His Son, the Lord Jesus. The source through which God, the heavenly Father of all, displays and applies His merciful forgiveness to the sins of mankind is the *blood of Christ*.

Paul expresses it clearly in Romans 5:8–9.

> *But God commendeth his love toward us, in that, while we were yet sinners, Christ died for us.*
>
> *Much more then, being now justified by his blood, we shall be saved from wrath through him.*

In this chosen manner of salvation, the Father unveils, through His spirit and spiritual words, the saving work of the blood of His Son. Jesus, as the One anointed by the Father, by means of His sacrificial obedience to the Father's method of salvation, sheds His blood and dies to cover the sins of Adam's fallen family.

The grace of God and the gift of grace are from the one human, Jesus Christ. It is available to Adam's many family members who are dying because of Adam's one offense, passing death to all (Romans 5:15).

The judgment of the penalty of death applies to all out of the condemnation from one act of sinning, whereas the gracious gift as a just award is out of many offenses (Romans 5:16).

The one offense has resulted in the reign of death over all humanity. But in a much greater manner, those obtaining the superabundance of grace and the free gift of righteousness shall reign through the one, Jesus Christ (Romans 5:17).

Consequently, then, even though by the means of the one offense all humans came under the condemnation, through one just award all humans come under the superabounding grace of the justification of life (Romans 5:18).

And, through the disobedience of the one human, Adam, all humans were constituted sinners, whereas, by the obedience of the one human, Jesus Christ, all shall be constituted just (Romans 5:19).

Paul presents the gospel, which saves those who hear and believe through the power of God. The covering over of sins is available to every person who is called by God to believe in the saving message.

All believers share God's forgiveness of sins by the blood of Christ in a common manner. That is, the blood answers to each individual separately to cover the sins of that person. Sins committed are linked to each sinner in an individual manner, as a member of Adam's fallen family.

Each person's sins are their own, and they are not related to any other sinful human. Each person in Old Humanity must account for their personal sins. No one can account for them except Jesus, the Son of Man, whose blood covers the sins of each sinner who comes to Him for cleansing.

A forgiven sinner shares a common faith with all other believers, having been justified by their blood. God sees each sinner now as a just saint when the blood of Christ is applied.

The blood of Jesus is the first element of Paul's gospel. The saving work of Christ has begun in the life of the new saint who has received the revelation of the blood's efficacy concerning the sins of the past.

One of the first people to receive a revelation of the saving work of Jesus received the holy baby at the Temple in Jerusalem. Jesus' human parents came to present Him, as reported by Luke in his gospel.

> *And, behold, there was a man in Jerusalem, whose name was Simeon; and the same man was just and devout, waiting for the consolation of Israel: and the Holy Ghost was upon him.*
>
> *And it was revealed unto him by the Holy Ghost, that he should not see death, before he had seen the Lord's Christ.*
>
> *And he came by the Spirit into the temple: and when the parents brought in the child Jesus, to do for him after the custom of the law,*
>
> *Then took he him up in his arms, and blessed God, and said,*
>
> *Lord, now lettest thou thy servant depart in peace, according to thy word:*
> *For mine eyes have seen thy salvation,*
> *Which thou hast prepared before the face of all people;*
> *A light to lighten the Gentiles, and the glory of thy people Israel.*
> *Luke 2:25-32*

In the phrase *"to lighten the Gentiles,"* Luke uses the word *apokalupsis*, which is a state, in this case, of unveiling the *"salvation"* of God. Simeon's eyes had gazed upon the baby Jesus, the Savior of all.

Simeon's literal physical eyes beheld the promise that the angel had given him as the exact answer to his prayer. His eyes saw the saving work (*soterion, G#4992, salvation*) of God in the child held in his arms.

The infant would become God's saving work, both to Israelites who would behold His glory and to Gentiles who received spiritual eyesight by means of the revelation of Him without seeing Him face to face.

Luke speaks of *soterion* again in chapter three of his gospel as he reports the beginning of the ministry of John the Baptist.

> *And he came into all the country about Jordan, preaching the baptism of repentance for the remission of sins;*
>
> *As it is written in the book of the words of Esaias the prophet, saying, The voice of one crying in the wilderness, Prepare ye the way of the Lord, make his paths straight.*
>
> *Every valley shall be filled, and every mountain and hill shall be brought low; and the crooked shall be made straight, and the rough ways shall be made smooth;*
>
> *And all flesh shall see the salvation of God. Luke 3:3-6*

In this last verse, Luke describes salvation (*soterion*), as he uses a new word for "seeing," which is *optanomai (Strong's #3700, a verb meaning to see with wide-open eyes, as at something remarkable)*.

All flesh shall see God's saving work accomplished in Christ Jesus. Believers who are currently called will witness a revelation and see with spiritual eyes. Those who do not receive such an *apokalupsis* will see with their physical eyes when brought before Him in His radiant glory.

Paul, in the closing verses of Acts, chapter 28, employs the same saving work, *soterion*, after his lengthy conversation with the Jewish elders residing in Rome concerning the Lord's ministry. Paul's proclamation and explanation concerning the saving work of Jesus fell on deaf ears as the majority of the listening elders of Israel residing in Rome turned away from his gospel message. However, a few were blessed with a revelation (Acts 28:24).

> *Be it known therefore unto you, that the salvation (soterion) of God is sent unto the Gentiles, and that they will hear it. Acts 28:28*

God's saving work, as accomplished in Christ Jesus, is a double-sided salvation. First, on the side of His ministry, from the baptism by John to His death on the cross, Jesus, as the Son of Man, nullified both sin and death, which affects all of humanity.

The other side of Christ's saving work is related to Israel, not to the Gentile nations directly. It is an accomplishment of His ministry to confirm the promises to Israel spoken in the past to the fathers of Israel's faith. (Romans 15:8).

Superseding His ministry to both Israel and the nations is the saving work of including all of humanity in His crucifixion, death, burial, and resurrection. This element of Christ's saving work transcends the *common* truth of justification in His blood, becoming a *joint* truth that applies to every person of Adam's race jointly, that is, bringing together and applying to all of humanity as an aggregate group.

The faith that God imparts to believers concerning these elements of the *joint* faith, when embraced and believed, breaks down the dividing partitions of separation between factions and sects within the professing church. Upon receipt of the joint truths, the unity of the spirit binds believers together, which must be maintained so as to walk in the worthy manner of their calling (Ephesians 4:1–3).

When Jesus was placed on the cross and nailed to the beams, all of humanity was in Him. When He died, the Old Humanity died with Him.

Likewise, when He was taken down and wrapped in burial clothes, all of Adam's family was included.

These joint truths are presented as a vital part of Paul's gospel in Romans 6:1 –10. There are no companion writings in the New Testament that present the joint truths that were revealed to Paul. It is fitting that these elements of the saving work of the Lord are included in our discussion.

Romans 6

1. What shall we say then? Shall we continue in sin so that grace may abound?

2. God forbid. How shall we, that are dead to sin, live any longer therein?

3. Know ye not that so many of us who were baptized into Jesus Christ were baptized into his death?

4. Therefore, we are buried with him by baptism into death: that like as Christ was raised up from the dead by the glory of the Father, even so we also should walk in newness of life.

5. For if we have been planted together in the likeness of his death, we shall be also in the likeness of his resurrection:

6. Knowing this, that our old man is crucified with him, that the body of sin might be destroyed, that henceforth we should not serve sin.

7. For he that is dead is freed from sin.

8. Now if we be dead with Christ, we believe that we shall also live with him:

> *9. Knowing that Christ being raised from the dead dieth no more; death hath no more dominion over him.*
>
> *10. For in that he died, he died unto sin once: but in that he liveth, he liveth unto God.*

There are four key joint words provided in this proclamation of Paul's description of Christ's saving work in Romans 6.

1. In vs. 4, entombed together, *sunthapto (Strong's #G4916)*
2. In vs. 5, planted together, *sumphutos (Strong's #G4854)*
3. In vs. 6, crucified together, *sustauroo (Strong's #G4957)*
4. In vs. 8, live together with him, *suzao (Strong's #G4800)*

All believers identified with Christ's blood when, by faith, they were individually justified and determined by God to not be guilty of their sins. His blood covering over the sins of the flesh is the common truth of Paul's evangel, the initial spiritual fact of the Lord's saving work.

Now, we must advance in the truth to take possession of additional "land" in this realm of God's grace. It is time to embrace the truths of Christ's saving work from both sin and death.

Jesus became sin on the cross.. He then entered into death. His identification with fallen humanity was complete.

The value of Christ's blood cannot be measured as it covers over the sins of each person who thanks God for its worth. The effectiveness of the mercy of God upon the fallen sinner has no counterpart in the saving work. It is justification for everyone who comes under the common fountain of God's bountiful grace.

The blood has finished its work concerning the sins of sinners. We now press on to identify with the Savior's death. These joint words relate to His body, applied in the death of His body, and our unification with Him, applied in the new life of Him in His resurrection.

Identification with the death of God's Son by the expression of faith in the above section of Paul's letter to the Romans is the necessary step towards Sonship.

In verses 4–6 of Chapter 6 of Romans, the Old Humanity (*palaios anthropos*) is that which our Lord and Savior thoroughly identified with when He was crucified. All humans, who obtain their physical body from Adam, are included in the Old Humanity.

As He identified with all of humanity in His overcoming life and his sacrificial death, all humans are called to identify with Him in His new life.

In verse 8, to live with Him, sharing in His life, we must be joined by faith to His death.

His cross is our cross. His death is our death. His life is our life.

When they took Him down from the cross, we all came down with Him. Then we were placed in his tomb. While in the tomb, He was given new life and a new body.

He was resurrected as the head of the church and the head of the New Humanity (*kainos anthropos*), the beginning of a new creation in Him.

We all, being in Him, share these spiritual truths together. These are joint truths, applying to all humans as a unit. No person is left out of His saving work. We are all included at the same time, during the same experience of Christ, and we must all see that the joint truths that Paul presents must be applied to all by faith in the operation of God (Colossians 2:12).

The Holy Spirit of God, residing in the hearts of the saints, administers the truths of His saving work - His blood and His body - to the believing members of His body, the church. The believers, now recognized as saints, were formerly fallen, dying sinners.

Faith begins as the gospel's words reveal the power of Christ's blood to cover a person's sins. Faith continues to grow as the believing saint proceeds in Paul's gospel to the cross of Christ. It is at the cross that He conquered both sin and death in His crucifixion.

It is in His resurrection that He was then declared to be God's Son with power, according to the spirit of holiness (Romans 1:4).

Moreover, when the Holy Spirit reveals the truths contained in Romans 6 to the believer, another facet of the jewel of revelation shines forth. The Spirit of God baptizes the believer into Christ by baptism into His death (Romans 6:3).

The unveiling (*apokalupsis*) of this truth is necessary to end the rule of sin in the believer's body. Because of sin that is in the human body that the body is here referred to as the *body of sin*. It is nullified due to the Old Humanity being crucified with Christ and put to death in Him (Romans 6:6).

The spiritual child of God now advances in faith, due to the joint resurrection. When He rises, all of humanity is resurrected in Him. A new young spiritual believer comes forth in the risen Lord.

The new convert does not know the details of God's saving work through Christ. What is known is that each person was an an unbelieving spiritually blind sinner, but when saving faith comes and is embraced, that person is now a spiritually sighted saint.

The spiritual young one must mature in faith. Whereas, prior to the unveiling of the truth in Romans 6, the believer was dominated by both the *soul* and the *flesh*. This condition Paul describes as *carnal and fleshly*.

The child of God is an heir awaiting the visible kingdom that will come at the proper time. But as long as the visible kingdom is impending, the Invisible kingdom's dominium is at work in the heart of man.

At the initial state of growth, the child *(nepios, Strong's #G3516, not speaking)* is in a condition of minority, an immature Christian. The minor child must be schooled in the language of God, using spiritual words and phrases taught by the Spirit of God.

In this era of the invisible Kingdom of God, God places His spirit within the believer so that spiritual growth may begin and proceed to a place of accomplishment *(teleios, Strong's #G5046, completeness, full age)*. It is the power of God that makes this possible. Believers being schooled in this manner express spiritual wisdom through spiritual words and phrases.

This spiritual wisdom is not understood by the world, as Paul explained in his first letter to the church at Corinth.

> *Now we have received, not the spirit of the world, but the spirit which is of God; that we might know the things that are freely given to us of God.*
>
> *Which things also we speak, not in the words which man's wisdom teacheth, but which the Holy Ghost teacheth; comparing spiritual things with spiritual. I Corinthians 2:12,13.*

Paul expresses that God wants the body of Christ to know those things that He has given to us. The Holy Spirit of God teaches us these things spiritually. These matters are spiritual *(pneumatikos, Strong's #G4152, an adjective meaning belonging to the Divine Spirit, one who is filled with and governed by the Spirit of God, in which the human spirit is elevated to a higher or renovated nature)*, which are the heavenly food for the spirit within the heart of each believer.

> *But the natural man receiveth not the things of the Spirit of God: for they are foolishness unto him: neither can he know them, because they are spiritually discerned. I Corinthians 2:14*

The *natural man* is soulish *(psuchikos, Strong's #G5591, an adjective describing a sensitive nature, subject to its appetites and passions)*. The natural man in this early state cannot receive the things of the spirit of God. The spiritual things, which he cannot accept, are foolishness to him. The ultimate goal is to become *pneumatikos (Strong's # G4153, an adverb that describes that which is spiritually attained with the aid of the Holy Spirit)*.

The next step is to challenge the realm of the *natural man*—the realm of the carnal mind. In the carnal mind, the focus of life is dominated by fleshly dictates and desires.

> *And I, brethren, could not speak unto you as unto spiritual but as unto carnal, even as unto babes in Christ. I Corinthians 3:1*

The carnal believer is still in the minority of faith but can be urged to move upward. To be carnal is fleshly *(fleshly, sarkikos, G#4559, one who is governed by the human fleshly nature and not by the Spirit of God)*. Paul claims that wherever divisions exist, there is strife and envy. Carnal believers *walk as men (I Corinthians 3:3)*.

> *Now I say, That the heir, as long as he is a child, differeth nothing from a servant, though he be lord of all;*
>
> *But is under tutors and governors until the time appointed of the father.*
>
> *Even so we, when we were children, were in bondage under the elements of the world:*

> *But when the fulness of the time was come, God sent forth his Son, made of a woman, made under the law,*
>
> *To redeem them that were under the law, that we might receive the adoption of sons.*
>
> *And because ye are sons, God hath sent forth the Spirit of his Son into your hearts, crying, Abba, Father.*
>
> *Wherefore thou art no more a servant, but a son; and if a son, then an heir of God through Christ. Galatians 4:1-7*

In a state of minority, the Christian child is no different from a slave of the household. A slave is a *doulos (Strong's #G1401, a servant in subjection and subservience)*. The child is subject to guardians and administrators until a designated day when the Father declares an advance into the realm of authority and responsibility in the household.

This common practice in the culture of Paul's day is descriptive of the process of spiritual maturity in the body of Christ. God, our heavenly Father, at the appropriate time, delegated Christ, His Son, on a mission of redemption.

Jesus was dispatched to reclaim humanity from the kingdom of darkness and transport the New Humanity into the kingdom of light, the Kingdom of God's Son (Colossians 1:13).

The struggle to bear fruit for God becomes a heartfelt goal of those of God's children who seek advancement from spiritual minority to elevation into the state of *sonship*. As the yearning believer moves from service to sin to the liberty of joining Christ on His cross through faith in Romans 6:6, the next step is to enter and pass through Romans, Chapter 7.

Because the young believer has seen the crucifixion of the Old Humanity with Christ and celebrates the victory over sin accomplished in Christ's obedience, a new perspective concerning the flesh must be developed in the mind.

Here's Paul's discovery:

> *But now we are delivered from the law, that being dead wherein we were held; that we should serve in newness of spirit, and not in the oldness of the letter.*
>
> *What shall we say then? Is the law sin? God forbid. Nay, I had not known sin, but by the law: for I had not known lust, except the law had said, Thou shalt not covet.*
>
> *But sin, taking occasion by the commandment, wrought in me all manner of concupiscence. For without the law sin was dead.*
>
> *For I was alive without the law once: but when the commandment came, sin revived, and I died.*
>
> *And the commandment, which was ordained to life, I found to be unto death.*
>
> *For sin, taking occasion by the commandment, deceived me, and by it slew me.*
>
> *Wherefore the law is holy, and the commandment holy, and just, and good.*
>
> *Was then that which is good made death unto me? God forbid. But sin, that it might appear sin, working death in me by that which is good; that sin by the commandment might become exceeding sinful. Romans 7:6-13*

Christ's victory over sin on the cross is our victory as well. He condemned sin in the flesh (Romans 8:3). As we are crucified with Him, we must identify with Him against sin, seeing that it is condemned. However, sin is not eliminated from our bodies yet. We become under its' rule again when we, in the flesh, attempt to bear fruit for God in our bodies, which Paul now refers to as *the body of this death (Romans 7:24)*.

Sin, in this case, works death in me by virtue of my vain attempt to serve God in the flesh. As I proceed in this vanity, *the law of sin* in my members is energized when I attempt to do good on God's behalf.

With the Lord's help through the Spirit, I am in need of a new revelation that will enlighten my mind to understand that I serve God's law with my mind, but with the flesh, the law of sin (Romans 7:25).

As the Spirit renews my mind, I am no longer a slave to sin, nor am I capable of bearing fruit on my own. I begin to identify with Christ's death as the Son of Man.

We must see ourselves in *Christ*. No longer are we to see ourselves *in the flesh*. We are to develop the Romans 8 mindset. *For they that are after the flesh do mind the things of the flesh; but they that are after the Spirit the things of the Spirit.*

> *For to be carnally minded is death; but to be spiritually minded is life and peace.*
>
> *Because the carnal mind is enmity against God: for it is not subject to the law of God, neither indeed can be.*
>
> *So then they that are in the flesh cannot please God. Romans 8:5-8*

The child of God in the minority is subject to both sin and death by means of *the law of sin and death (Romans 8:2)*. The revelation that we are *in the spirit* is contained in *Romans 8:9*.

> *But ye are not in the flesh, but in the Spirit, if so be that the Spirit of God dwell in you. Now if any man have not the Spirit of Christ, he is none of his. The law of the spirit of the life in Christ Jesus* operative within us.

As the Spirit of God dwells in us, we are *not in the flesh*. The indwelling Spirit becomes to us *the Spirit of Christ* as the renewal of our minds progresses, bringing us into a new way of seeing things from a spiritual point of view. The new law in us nullifies sin's law that produces death.

> *For ye have not received the spirit of bondage again to fear; but ye have received the Spirit of adoption, whereby we cry, Abba, Father. Romans 8:15*

The Holy Spirit is communicating to our spirit, the spiritual man in our hearts, that we are now sharing a bond of sonship with our heavenly Father that previously we didn't know. We are the spiritual children of God who now enjoy a new relationship. We are sons of God.

> *The Spirit itself beareth witness with our spirit, that we are the children of God: And if children, then heirs; heirs of God, and joint-heirs with Christ; if so be that we suffer with him, that we may be also glorified together. Romans 8:16,17*

There are four *sun* words in the previous two verses. The eighth chapter of Romans is replete with words of unity from Paul. We will discuss these four words here, while the remaining words of unity in Romans 8 will be addressed later in the appropriate section of this manuscript.

The first of the *sun* words is found in the phrase, *The Spirit itself beareth witness with our spirit*. We find the Greek word *summartureo (Strong's #G4828, to testify jointly, to bear joint witness)*. In our early stages of believing, we may not have had a witness of the Spirit, but rather the witness of the Word, having been told beforehand that we are offspring of God. In this verse, our spirit, along with a joint witness by God's Spirit, produces certainty in our inner man.

The second *sun* word is found in the phrase, *And if children, then heirs; heirs of God, and joint-heirs with Christ*. Paul tells us here that as offspring of God, we are *heirs of God*. We all have an inheritance awaiting our son placing *(huiosthesia)*. Greater still is the privilege of being a *joint heir with Christ*. The word of unity here is *sunkleronomos (Strong's #G4789, a fellow heir, one who obtains something assigned to himself with others, a joint participant)*.

The third *sun* word qualifies the previous phrase conditionally. To be a *joint heir*, a believer has to *suffer with him*, which is a joint word, *sumpascho (Strong's #G4841, to experience pain jointly or of the same kind, especially persecution, suffer with)*. I believe that this recognizes the suffering of a higher level than that of a common believer in Jesus. An example of such suffering would be found in the life and ministry of Paul.

The fourth and final *sun* word in this section of Romans, chapter 8, is found in the closing words of verse 17, *that we may also be glorified together*. The word used by Paul is *sundoxazo (to exalt dignity in company with; also, to join in approving)*. All believers will be subject to glory in company with all other believers. It seems also that certain members of His body who suffered on a higher level due to extreme persecution will be afforded more magnificent glory.

How, or when, will this recognition be made?

It is appropriate that when God's Son, Jesus Christ, divested Himself from His heavenly glory and took upon the human form to come to earth and fulfill His glorious mission, God highly exalted Him and gave Him a name above all names. It is revealed by Paul to the church at Phillippi.

> *Let this mind be in you, which was also in Christ Jesus:*
>
> *Who, being in the form of God, thought it not robbery to be equal with God:*
>
> *But made himself of no reputation, and took upon him the form of a servant, and was made in the likeness of men:*
>
> *And being found in fashion as a man, he humbled himself, and became obedient unto death, even the death of the cross.*
>
> *Wherefore God also hath highly exalted him, and given him a name which is above every name:*
>
> *That at the name of Jesus every knee should bow, of things in heaven, and things in earth, and things under the earth; Phillippians 2:5-10*

This holy advice is directed to all of us who have been called by God to be a part of the divine work of salvation by God's only begotten Son, our Lord and Savior, Jesus Christ.

As we partake of the heavenly calling, we should keep in mind that the way that we walk in this world will be subjected to the searching eye of the Lord when we are joined to Him when He returns to claim us as His own.

> *Therefore we are always confident, knowing that, whilst we are at home in the body, we are absent from the Lord:*
>
> *(For we walk by faith, not by sight:)*
>
> *We are confident, I say, and willing rather to be absent from the body, and to be present with the Lord.*

THE IDENTIFICATION OF HUMANITY WITH CHRIST

Wherefore we labour, that, whether present or absent, we may be accepted of him.

For we must all appear before the judgment seat of Christ; that every one may receive the things done in his body, according to that he hath done, whether it be good or bad.

Knowing therefore the terror of the Lord, we persuade men; but we are made manifest unto God; and I trust also are made manifest in your consciences. II Corinthians 5:6-11

God, the Father, has joined the Old Humanity with Christ, as the Son of Man, in His saving work. In the words of unity in Chapter 6 of Romans, we discover our inclusion in Him. We have also discussed that when He was brought back to life, the New Humanity was created in Him while still in the tomb.

He is now the risen New Man, who has ascended into heaven to return to call His body on earth to Himself.

Jesus is the perfect man who was worthy through His perfect life as the Lamb of God to be sacrificed for the redemption of Adam's fallen family. In that capacity, He poured out His soul in His shed blood, took upon Himself the sin that Adam allowed into the creation, received the sentence of death meant for all people, and died upon the cross.

In that divine process, Jesus Christ represented the Old Humanity in its entirety through His crucifixion, death, and entombment.

The Father, by the power of His Spirit, raised His Son from the dead, creating the New Humanity in Him. The New Creation is advancing. He is making all things new.

As the resurrection companies arise, as described in I Corinthians 15, separate segments of humanity will come forth into the new life that is in Christ.

Believers are to grow in grace and the knowledge of Christ, being conformed to His image, until the next company, which are those that are His at His coming, is called forth. *But now is Christ risen from the dead, and become the firstfruits of them that slept.*

> *For since by man came death, by man came also the resurrection of the dead.*
>
> *For as in Adam all die, even so in Christ shall all be made alive.*
>
> *But every man in his own order: Christ the firstfruits; afterward they that are Christ's at his coming.*
>
> *Then cometh the end, when he shall have delivered up the kingdom to God, even the Father; when he shall have put down all rule and all authority and power.*
>
> *For he must reign, till he hath put all enemies under his feet.*
>
> *The last enemy that shall be destroyed is death. I Corinthians 15:20-26*

Jesus, as the Son of man, came into the first creation to undo that which the Adversary had caused through Adam, the first man, by the entry of both sin and death.

Jesus did not come to repair, restore, or rehabilitate the *Old Humanity*.

> *He that committeth sin is of the devil; for the devil sinneth from the beginning. For this purpose, the Son of God was manifested, that he might destroy the works of the devil. I John 3:8*

Jesus came to end the Old and create the New.

It is our responsibility to believe in His accomplishments by entering into His saving work and allowing His Spirit to work through us.

Good works are the goal before us, as Paul wrote to the church at Ephesus.

> *For we are his workmanship, created in Christ Jesus unto good works, which God hath before ordained that we should walk in them. Ephesians 2:10*

and to His fellow worker, Timothy.

> *That the man of God may be perfect, thoroughly furnished unto all good works. II Timothy 3:17*

While we await the Lord's return, let us join together in a pursuit of truth, which I called *Chasing Truth*. This heavenly quest is, without doubt, the most important endeavor of our lives.

When He returns, the last thing that we want to happen is to be ashamed of our journey's pursuit.

Paul admonished his close associates in this wise way:

> *Wherefore we labour, that, whether present or absent, we may be accepted of him.*
>
> *For we must all appear before the judgment seat of Christ; that everyone may receive the things done in his body, according to that he hath done, whether it be good or bad.*

> *Knowing therefore the terror of the Lord, we persuade men; but we are made manifest unto God; and I trust also are made manifest in your consciences.*
>
> *For we commend not ourselves again unto you, but give you occasion to glory on our behalf, that ye may have somewhat to answer them which glory in appearance, and not in heart.*
>
> *For whether we be beside ourselves, it is to God: or whether we be sober, it is for your cause.*
>
> *For the love of Christ constraineth us; because we thus judge, that if one died for all, then were all dead:*
>
> *And that he died for all, that they which live should not henceforth live unto themselves, but unto him which died for them, and rose again.*
> *II Corinthians 5:9-15*

The judgment seat of Christ is not a place of condemnation. For there is no condemnation for those who are in Christ Jesus (Romans 8:1). It is a raised platform from which recognition will be made for those who have conducted themselves in an exemplary manner in their walk with Christ.

A worthy walk is by one who bears with others in love, with all lowliness and meekness, with suffering (Ephesians 4:1–2).

It bears repeating that in Christ there is a new law operating in us by the empowerment of God's spirit acting upon our spirit, the inner man (Romans 8:2). The written law of God cannot produce life in us. When we attempt to obey the law of God with our flesh, empowerment is provided to the law in our flesh, the law of sin and death.

The new law that will produce within us a desire to please God and is the source of His love to be shared with others is *the law of the spirit of life in Christ Jesus hath made me free from the law of sin and death.*

CHAPTER 4

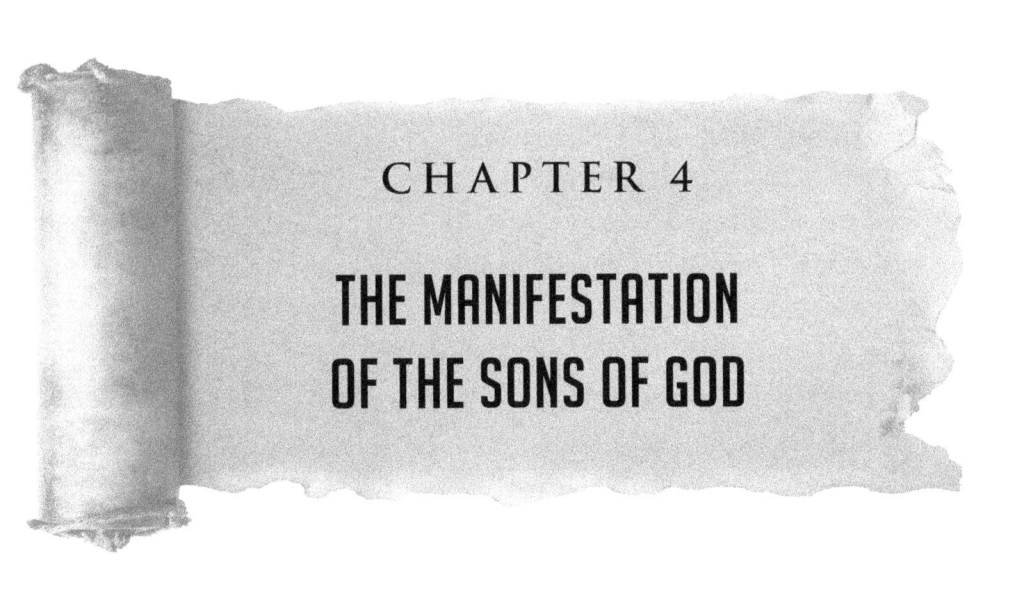

THE MANIFESTATION OF THE SONS OF GOD

THE UNITY BETWEEN GOD, THE FATHER, GOD, THE SON AND THE NEW MAN

We have now arrived at the central purpose of this manuscript. Thank you for taking this journey with me. Humanity has suffered many long and exhausting challenges. As Jesus proclaimed, there will be wars and rumors of wars.

Human history is replete with struggles. Divisions within the world abound. Nations conflict with other nations. Even at the lowest level of civilization, people clash with each other as they attempt to gain the meager, rudimentary provisions of existence.

The question is often posed: Where is God? Why are we subject to this seemingly vain and agonizing grief?

Surely, our Creator brought forth this creation for a special purpose, of which we all play a part. There must be a purpose for it all.

In what often seems like a hopeless future, we learn in His scripture that the end does, in fact, justify the means. In the end, evil will be overcome by good.

At the very beginning of the first creation, darkness prevailed. God's first act was to speak forth light, and there was light. At this later hour, this age seems to have entered its twilight. But there is a different kind of darkness that has enveloped the nations. Both Isaiah and Jeremiah spoke of this time.

> *For, behold, the darkness shall cover the earth and the gross darkness the people; but the Lord shall arise upon thee, and his glory shall be seen upon thee. Isaiah 60:2*
>
> *Give glory to the Lord your God, before he causes darkness and before your feet stumble upon the dark mountains, and while ye look for light, he turns it into the shadow of death and makes it gross darkness. Jeremiah 13:16*

Light dispels darkness. Jesus said of Himself that He was the light of the world.

> *Then Jesus spoke again unto them, saying, I am the light of the world; he that followeth me shall not walk in darkness, but shall have the light of life. John 8:12*

He also said of His followers that they were also in the world to be light.

> *Ye are the light of the world. A city that is set on a hill cannot be hidden. Matthew 5:14*

Spiritual darkness covers the hearts of those who have been blinded by God's adversary. Paul explains this in his letter to the church at Corinth.

> *But if our gospel is hidden, it is hidden to those who are lost. In whom the god of this world hath blinded the minds of those who believe not, lest the light of the glorious gospel of Christ, who is the image of God, shine unto them. II Corinthians 4:3–4*

The gospel that Paul proclaimed is a message of good news. It contains the power of God to save humanity, bringing believers into its wondrous light. The gospel concerns Jesus, as He is the light of the world.

Paul adds more information in the same letter.

> *For such are false apostles, deceitful workers, transforming themselves into the apostles of Christ.*
>
> *And no marvel, for Satan himself is transformed into an angel of light.*
>
> *Therefore, it is no great thing if his ministers also be transformed into ministers of righteousness, whose end shall be according to their works. II Corinthians 11:13–15*

Satan is transformed into an angel of light, disguising and transfiguring himself on the outside. This altered appearance is an outward ruse. It is not a genuine external change coming from an internal light. The word for this transformation is *metaschematizo (Strong's #G3345, to transfigure or disguise)*.

This disguise contrasts with the genuine external change that will occur when Jesus Christ returns to claim His body on earth, as Paul explains to the church in Philippi.

> *Who shall change our vile body so that it may be fashioned like his glorious body according to the working whereby he is able even to subdue all things unto himself? Philippians 3:21*

Satan's exterior change is false. The change in the body of believers who are the Lord's at His appearing is true and real.

Jesus is the true light. Satan falsely changes his figure.

As the adversary continuously blinds the minds of people to the liberty of the gospel, the insidious work is enhanced by the counterfeit message of salvation.

We should not, however, credit the adversary unduly for these deceptive abilities, as if his strategies have provided unlimited application. Our God is sovereign. He allows the enemy to use these abilities under certain conditions and limitations.

In his second letter to the church at Thessalonica, Paul provides additional information on the workings of spiritual darkness. Again, it is important that we recognize that the forces of evil in the kingdom of darkness are not given total freedom of operation. God places boundaries that limit the deception.

A chief feature of Satan's deception will be to counter the manifestation of the Sons of God. He will manifest the Son of perdition as Paul described in his second letter to the church at Thessalonica.

> *Now we beseech you, brethren, by the coming of our Lord Jesus Christ and by our gathering together unto him,*

That ye be not soon shaken in mind or troubled, neither by spirit nor by word nor by letter as from us, as that the day of Christ is at hand. Let no man deceive you by any means, for that day shall not come, except there come a falling away first, and that man of sin be revealed, the son of perdition;

Who opposeth and exalteth himself above all that is called God, or that is worshipped, so that he, as God, sitteth in the temple of God, showing himself that he is God? Remember, ye not, that, when I was yet with you, I told you these things?

And now ye know what withholdeth that he might be revealed in his time. II Thessalonians 2:1–6

The church at Thessalonica had grown exceedingly in faith. Their love for each other abounded. Paul, Silvanus, and Timothy reported these special characteristics of spiritual maturity to the other churches they visited. No one has such an overcoming beginning. Faith must mature and grow.

In his first letter to this notable church, Paul had to encourage them that their trials were not evidence of the imminent return of the Lord. They were under extreme persecution for their faith, which caused them to reason that the Day of the Lord had arrived, leaving them amid God's wrath. But Paul encouraged them accordingly.

For if we believe that Jesus died and rose again, even so, those who sleep in Jesus will God bring with him.

For this we say unto you by the word of the Lord, that we which are alive and remain unto the coming of the Lord shall not prevent them which are asleep.

> *For the Lord himself shall descend from heaven with a shout, with the voice of the archangel, and with the trump of God, and the dead in Christ shall rise first:*
>
> *Then we which are alive and remain shall be caught up together with them in the clouds, to meet the Lord in the air, and so shall we ever be with the Lord. I Thessalonians 4:14–17*

Further, in the same letter, Paul consoled the anxious believers in Thessalonica with comforting words.

> *For God hath not appointed us to wrath, but to obtain salvation by our Lord Jesus Christ, I Thessalonians 5:9*

Paul assured them that even though many of their fellow believers had fallen asleep and been placed in graves, the dead in Christ would rise first at His appearing, followed by those still alive at His coming. They were unaware at that time that the entire body of Christ would be snatched away at the same time.

Paul had also revealed to the church at Corinth the secret of the miraculous delivery that would take place at the end of this current age.

> *Behold, I shew you a mystery: We shall not all sleep, but we shall all be changed.*
>
> *In a moment, in the twinkling of an eye, at the last trump: for the trumpet shall sound, and the dead shall be raised incorruptible, and we shall be changed. I Corinthians 15:51–52*

In his second letter to the saints in Thessalonica, a sequel to the first letter he sent to them, Paul provided detailed information concerning conditions in the world that would be evidence of the coming of God's wrath. He explained specific events that must precede the Day of Christ. He warned them not to be deceived by false reports.

He informed them, and to us as well, who read and heeded his letters, that the great falling away from the faith would occur that would open the door for entry into the world of the man of sin, the false Christ.

> *For the mystery of iniquity doth already work: only he who now letteth will let, until he is taken out of the way.*
>
> *And then shall that Wicked be revealed, whom the Lord shall consume with the spirit of his mouth and shall destroy with the brightness of his coming:*
>
> *Even he, whose coming is after the working of Satan with all power, signs, and lying wonders,*
>
> *And with all deceivableness and unrighteousness in them, they perish because they received not the love of the truth, that they might be saved.*
>
> *And for this cause, God shall send them strong delusion that they should believe a lie.*
>
> *That they all might be damned who believed not the truth but had pleasure in unrighteousness. II Thessalonians 2:7-12*

To those who are seeking spiritual growth towards the goal of maturity, Paul exhorted that all believers recognize that God is sending *strong delusion* to those that do not receive *the love of the truth*. Paul explains that for those who do not receive this special grace of God's love, it may be possible that *they should believe a lie* from the *wicked* one. If so, they might embrace the false gospel and the miraculous exhibition of power from Satan that will enthrall the unsuspecting masses.

There is a spiritual dynamism that is keeping the lawless one from being openly manifested. When this divine vitality is withdrawn, an era of unprecedented deception will come forth in its fullness.

Could the love of the truth, transmitted through the Spirit of God to the sons of God who await His return, serve as the restraining force? The gospel of Paul, as proclaimed in his second letter to the Thessalonians, directs God's children accordingly.

> *But we are bound to give thanks always to God for you, brethren beloved of the Lord, because God hath from the beginning chosen you to salvation through sanctification of the Spirit and belief in the truth.*
>
> *Whereunto he called you by our gospel, to the obtaining of the glory of our Lord Jesus Christ.*
>
> *Therefore, brethren, stand fast and hold the traditions that ye have been taught, whether by word or our epistle.*
>
> *Now our Lord Jesus Christ himself, and God, even our Father, which hath loved us and hath given us everlasting consolation and good hope through grace,*
>
> *Comfort your hearts and establish you in every good word and work. II Thessalonians 2:13–17*

Paul's gospel is the purifying element that sanctifies. Whereas the false gospel and misleading teachings of deceitful workers veil the mind from the truth. The result is an empty religion filled with fleshly wisdom and works, resulting in itching ears and slothful attitudes that are a reproach to God.

God's purpose and desire for the sons of God is to be in unity with Him and His Son and in unity with each other through the gospel entrusted to

Paul. In the first creation, the unity between the Lord God and man was short-lived. The body of believers that are in the new creation in Christ currently enjoys peace, consolation, and joy where unity prevails.

When unity initially existed between God and Adam, the first human displayed marvelous abilities. Adam was able to converse with God, to listen to Him, and to receive the instructions necessary to carry out his specified duties, which were to dress and keep the garden.

Adam immediately exhibited the ability to talk and to think. When he was made aware that he needed another to help him and the animals of the creation were brought before him, he named each of them but found none of them as equipped and able to help him. How can we appreciate the superior functionality of his mind to accomplish such a feat? There remained another, not yet revealed, who would be his helper.

The marvelous gift of God to Adam was his mate, who would be joined to him in a holy bond. They were to function together in unbreakable unity.

As previously discussed, the chief adversary of God came forth to turn man away from God, seeming to disrupt His divine purpose. The subtle creature spoke deceptive, enticing words that they acted upon, dividing the fallen couple from their Creator.

In this latter day, the enemy's threat is even more relentless and pervasive as the works to deceive Adam's entire family have reached an ominous level. Paul asserted that this time the enemy would ultimately fail as the Lord would appear, silencing the fallen deceitful foe.

Unity between the Lord God and Adam, along with Adam's mate, Eve, was God's supreme goal for His human family. To be in unity with Him, they were to heed His instructions and follow His guidance.

During the transgression in the garden and the resulting estrangement between the Lord God and His created children, unity was broken, replaced by division from God and hostility caused by the curses upon the three participants in the rebellion.

> *For Adam was first formed, then Eve.*
>
> *And Adam was not deceived, but the woman being deceived was in the transgression. I Timothy 2:13-14*

Eve's transgression was not being subjected to Adam. She acted without seeking his advice.

The disobedience of Adam was due to a lack of heed for the words God gave him. Paul uses a special word to describe it.

> *For as by one man's disobedience many were made sinners, so by the obedience of one shall many be made righteous. Romans 5:19*

The word for *disobedience* in this verse is *parakoe (Strong's #G3876, to hear amiss)*. God's instructions concerning the fruit of the tree of the knowledge of good and evil were exact. They were neither complicated nor hard to understand.

Adam's sin affected and damaged the entire creation. It was due primarily to not listening attentively. His mate, Eve, listened instead to the devious liar, speaking enticing words. Although not deceived, Adam still joined her in the transgression.

Note that *the obedience of one* (the Lord Jesus) results in righteousness. In this case, Jesus listened to the Father's instructions with an exactness that resulted in His saving work. Obedience, in this case, is *hupakoe (Strong's #G5218, obedience rendered to anyone's counsels, from a root word, hupakouo, which means to listen or to harken to a command)*.

Paul also uses *parakoe* in his second letter to the church at Corinth.

> *And having the readiness to revenge all disobedience when your obedience is fulfilled. II Corinthians 10:6*

Unity between the Lord God and His Son, Jesus Christ, has always been their bond, which ensures agreement and harmony between them. The Father always knew that His Son would listen to Him and heed His guidance and instruction. Likewise, the Son always knew that the Father would hear His prayers and respond accordingly.

In this latter day, believers in Christ must attentively hear the saving message of Paul's gospel, which focuses on the Son of God, Jesus, our Lord. The Father has spoken through His Son. We must heed the words.

This was Jesus' testimony in the gospel of John. His prayer to the Father perfectly displays the unity between them.

> *Sanctify them through thy truth; thy word is truth.*
>
> *As thou hast sent me into the world, even so have I also sent them into the world.*
>
> *And for their sakes, I sanctify myself so that they too might be sanctified through the truth.*
>
> *Neither pray I for these alone, but for them also, who shall believe in me through their word;*
>
> *That they all may be one; as thou, Father, art in me, and I in thee, that they also may be one in us; that the world may believe that thou hast sent me.*

> *And the glory which thou gavest me, I have given them; that they may be one, even as we are one.*
>
> *I in them, and thou in me, that they may be made perfect in one, and that the world may know that thou hast sent me and hast loved them, as thou hast loved me.*
>
> *Father, I will that they also, whom thou hast given me, be with me where I am; that they may behold my glory, which thou hast given me, for thou lovedst me before the foundation of the world. John 17:17-24*

Jesus' John 17 prayer to the Father is the picture-perfect prayer that visualizes humanity as one with the Father, with the Son, and with each other. The glory that emanates from unity is the divine expression that Jesus displayed on the mount of transfiguration.

> *And after six days, Jesus taketh Peter, James, and John, his brother, and bringeth them up into a high mountain apart.*
>
> *And was transfigured before them, and his face did shine as the sun, and his raiment was white as the light. Matthew 17:1-2*

It is His glory that He set aside when He humbled Himself and made Himself of no reputation, taking on the form of a servant, finding Himself in the fashion of a man (Philippians 2:7-8).

As Jesus has ascended into heaven after His crucifixion, death, and resurrection, regaining the glory of His heavenly person, the members of His body are to fully identify with Him in His ascension and current ministry in the heavenlies. They are anticipating the glory of their collective manifestation, their sonship (Romans 8:23)

Where He is, the church, as His body, is there with Him because the body is in Him. On earth, while He remains in heaven, He is in the body of each believing member through God's spirit dwelling within them.

He is the total and complete body of the New Humanity. All of the new creation and all creatures are in Him. They simply are not aware of this wondrous truth. As is true of all spiritual truth, each facet must be received and joined by faith.

Identification by the members of the body with Christ as the Son of Man, is the truth that links each member to His fulfillment and responsibility to come to earth to be joined to us. The members of his body are to be uniquely aware that they are the first company of humanity entering into the unity that the gospel of Paul provides.

He completely identified with humanity in His earthly role. We, as believers, are to know the truth of His identification and be joined by the identification that faith provides.

Believers should attach themselves to each other in the ever-expanding truth of our union with Him. As the knowledge of Him increases, identification with Him becomes a spiritual reality.

Members of the body of Christ are to see that Jesus, as the Son of Man, came to take humanity to the cross with Him as The Old Humanity. Consequently, all humans were in Him and were crucified with Him (Romans 6:6).

The spiritual principle behind this truth is found in the understanding that Adam's transgression led to sin entering and affecting all humans, and through sin, death passed to all of Adam's posterity. All humans were with Adam in the garden.

> *For as in Adam all die, even so in Christ shall all be made alive.*
> *I Corinthians 15:22*

Consequently, the same principle holds true for Jesus Christ. The Old Humanity began with Adam and ended with the crucified Christ. The New Humanity began with the risen Christ being joined to Him and to each other. In Him, *all shall be made alive (zoopoieo, Strong's #G2227, to revitalize).*

Jesus Christ will revitalize every human being when His saving work is completed. This truth can be understood in contrast to the spiritual truth expressed through Adam. Through him, all humans die because they were in him when He began to die.

As we perceive our union in Christ Jesus as He died, we are also to perceive that we were baptized into Him by the Spirit, baptized into His death (Romans 6:3), and are included in the New Humanity as He was brought back into life in the tomb.

All humans will be made alive because the New Humanity was revitalized in the tomb of Christ and brought forth in His resurrection.

> *Even when we were dead in sins, He hath quickened us together with Christ (by grace ye are saved). Ephesians 2:5*

Grace was expressed in the blood that Christ shed on Calvary. Grace was voiced again when He was nailed to the cross. Grace was conveyed when He died and was placed in the grave, the tomb of Joseph of Arimathea. Grace was pronounced when He was raised from the dead and rose again as the New Humanity.

Now we know from Paul's gospel that we were all revitalized together with Christ, *suzoopoieo (Strong's #G4806, to make one alive together).* This is grace on a higher level. Revitalizing together means that all humans, who have sinned and died in Adam, are revitalized collectively in Christ.

Paul expresses this truth again in his letter to the Colossians.

> *And you, being dead in your sins and the uncircumcision of your flesh, hath he quickened together (suzoopoieo) with him, having forgiven you all trespasses; Colossians 2:13*

In this uplifting companion truth to Ephesians 2:5, Paul expands on the former state of our separation from God by stating that our flesh was in an unclean state, characterized by *uncircumcision*. The sins and trespasses of the flesh of the Old Humanity placed all of humanity into the same status as the unclean of Israel. When all of the New Humanity was revitalized in Christ, every person was forgiven of all trespasses.

The state of uncleanness is where all of humanity, by virtue of the uncleanness of the flesh, remains until each individual expresses thankfulness and appreciation to God for His saving work in Jesus. To remain *in the flesh* is to remain in the spiritual condition of the *uncircumcision of the flesh*.

God has further changed our human condition of uncleanness by being in Christ. Paul expressed the truth of this in his letter to the Colossians.

> *In whom also ye are circumcised with the circumcision made without hands, in putting off the body of the sins of the flesh by the circumcision of Christ. Colossians 2:11*

That is amazing grace.

This *circumcision* is an inward condition, a work of God upon the heart of the believer who embraces this truth and is joined to it by faith.

As is applicable to all spiritual truth, believers are to be interconnected directly with each facet of truth by the gift of faith that God provides and to which His spirit bears witness. When we are joined to Him, we are joined to each other and to all others. There can be no division in His body.

Jesus is now, as the Son of man, the head of the New Humanity of which all who belong to Him are members of His body, the church. He will return to earth as the Son of man to put under His feet all that oppose God by opposition to the truth, lacking an attentive hearing of the gospel proclaimed by Paul.

Let us summarize again that portion of Paul's letter to the Romans, chapter 6, in which our glorious inclusion in His saving work begins to unfold.

> *What shall we say, then? Shall we continue in sin so that grace may abound? God forbid. How shall we, that are dead to sin, live any longer therein?*
>
> *Know ye not that so many of us who were baptized into Jesus Christ were baptized into his death?*
>
> *Therefore, we are buried with him by baptism into death, just as Christ was raised up from the dead by the glory of the Father; even so, we should also walk in the newness of life. For if we have been planted together in the likeness of his death, we shall also be in the likeness of his resurrection.*
>
> *Knowing this, that our old man is crucified with him, that the body of sin might be destroyed, and that henceforth we should not serve sin.*
>
> *For he who is dead is freed from sin. Now if we are dead with Christ, we believe that we shall also live with him.*

> *Knowing that Christ, being raised from the dead, dieth no more; death hath no more dominion over him.*
>
> *For in that he died, he died unto sin once; but in that he liveth, he liveth unto God. Romans 6:1-10*

I have repeated this section of Paul's letter to the Romans as it sets forth the foundation of the words of unity that reveal humanity's inclusion with Him in the process of the death of God's Son on the cross. God's Son, as the only one begotten by virtue of His unique birth, became the Son of man.

As the Son of man, Christ thoroughly identified with all of Adam's family in the Old Humanity as He suffered, was made to be sin, and died. We, as believers, knowing that we are part of humanity, are to be aware of our inclusion in Christ.

As such, we are a part of the unique company included in His death in God's declaration through Paul. We realize that we have been baptized into His death. By having faith in God's operation, we declare that we have been united with Christ in His saving work.

Those in the world who do not know of the Lord's inclusive saving work remain ignorant of the blessings. They cannot thank God for these magnificent gifts. Those of His body, however, are encouraged to embrace the truths of Paul's gospel and press on to the high calling of God in Christ Jesus (Philippians 3:14).

As members of the Old Humanity, when He died, we died as well. Faith links us to these joint truths. We are joined by Him. Believers identify with Adam as a part of the Old Humanity and are to identify with Christ as to His role as the Son of Man.

As a representative of Adam's family, Jesus, as the last Adam (I Corinthians 15:45b), defeated both sin and death through His obedience to the Father on His cross. We, as being in Adam, are included in the crucifixion and in His death.

We are also to identify with Him in the New Humanity as risen from the dead in Him. Christ, our Lord, is the second man from heaven (I Corinthians 15:47b).

The believing members of His body are to follow Paul as he presents his gospel truth. Acquiring knowledge of the truth is the first step. Then, by the sequential unfolding of each facet of Christ's saving work, the Lord links each believer, by witness, of the Holy Spirit's written words of truth revealed by Paul.

The gospel elements, containing the power of God for salvation, are to become the catalyst for spiritual growth, as Paul asserted in Romans, Chapter 1;

> *[16] For I am not ashamed of the gospel of Christ, for it is the power of God unto salvation to everyone that believeth, to the Jew first, and also to the Greek.*
>
> *[17] For therein is the righteousness of God revealed from faith to faith: as it is written, The just shall live by faith.*

He identified with us. We are to identify with Him. The joint identification truths follow the revelation of the blood of Christ covering the sins of each individual believer as the beginning of salvation through faith.

The person in the gospels who identified with Him the closest before the crucifixion was the lady who appeared in Simon the leper's house in Matthew 26.

> *Now when Jesus was in Bethany, in the house of Simon the leper,*
>
> *There came unto him a woman having an alabaster box of very precious ointment, and she poured it on his head as he sat at meat.*
>
> *But when his disciples saw it, they had indignation, saying, To "what purpose is this waste?"*
>
> *For this ointment might have been sold for much and given to the poor.*
>
> *When Jesus understood it, he said unto them, Why trouble ye the woman? for she hath wrought a good work upon me.*
>
> *For ye have the poor always with you, but me ye have not always.*
>
> *For in that she poured this ointment on my body, she did it for my burial.*
>
> *Verily, I say unto you, wheresoever this gospel shall be preached in the whole world, there shall also be this, that this woman hath done, be told for a memorial of her. Matthew 26:6-13*

The woman totally identified with the mission of Christ. His indignant disciples could not join with her in the selfless act. They saw it as a waste of something valuable that, if sold, could be given to the poor.

Jesus understood the magnanimous gesture and upbraided the callous disciples. He asked them why they were observing her act as an unfavorable excess. It was as if they were identifying with the poor, failing to identify with Him in His imminent departure from them.

The insightful woman ascertained that He would soon be put to death. He had clearly told His followers that the fateful day was upon Him, but they were not of the same mind with her. She was pouring out the oil on His body, which would soon be offered up as the ultimate sacrifice.

Could she have envisioned not only His death but her death in Him as well?

Her special act was of such overwhelming importance that Jesus saw it as the perfect act to represent the message of the gospel. Jesus wanted her act to serve as a fitting memorial wherever and whenever the gospel was presented in the whole world.

I believe that His response to the disciples concerning her was because she perceived the meaning of His sacrificial death, whereas they were blind to the symbolic meaning of preparing Him for burial.

Throughout the Old Testament, memorials were used to bring to mind noteworthy events that would identify the current observer with those of the past whose memories should be called to mind.

Memorials are reminders. Any worthy remembrance should link the present with the past.

Jewish history and the oracles of the Old Testament are replete with memorial events.

There is a glorious future event foretold by Paul, the Apostle to the nations, that will magnify the resurrection of Christ. God, the Father, will be glorified in the new bodies of His children, who are the second company of the resurrection, with Jesus being the firstfruit. This is the event in which God's sons will be glorified.

This will be the manifestation of the sons of God, the Sonship that Christ's Body awaits.

Those who belong to Christ Jesus at His appearing will receive the heavenly promise that is currently guaranteed by the presence of God's Spirit in believers' hearts. Jesus is the first fruit of the resurrection. He is the first one resurrected from the dead who was made into a life-giving spirit.

The company of believers who belong to Him will be the second company of the resurrection when He returns to claim them unto Himself. This vital portion of I Corinthians 15 is well worth repeating.

> *For if in this life only we have hope in Christ, we are of all men most miserable.*
>
> *But now Christ has risen from the dead and become the firstfruits of those who slept.*
>
> *For since by man came death, by man also came the resurrection of the dead.*
>
> *In Adam, all die; in Christ, all are made alive.*
>
> *But every man in his own order: Christ the firstfruits; afterwards, they that are Christ's at his coming.*
>
> *Then cometh the end, when he shall have delivered up the kingdom to God, even the Father, when he shall have put down all rule and all authority and power.*
>
> *For he must reign till he hath put all enemies under his feet.*
> *I Corinthians 15:19-25*

The end, spoken of here, is not the culmination of all things and of all history, but the consummation of the process of God in restoring all things.

He, with Christ as the head of the body, will end the history of the Old Humanity, and inaugurate the future of His fellowship with His new creation and with the new humanity.

The manifestation of the sons of God will be realized in the resurrection, which is the second resurrection after the resurrection of Christ. He represented the first fruits, risen from the dead in His new body. This second resurrection company is jointly made alive in a new body, joining Him as His helpers and fellow workers, representing to the creation their grand mission as manifested sons of God.

This is the glorious hope of the members of the body of Christ, which will be fully realized according to the prophecy delivered by Paul in the form of a prayer in his letter to those in Ephesus called saints.

> *Therefore, after I heard of your faith in the Lord Jesus and your love for all the saints, Cease not to give thanks for you, making mention of you in my prayers;*
>
> *That the God of our Lord Jesus Christ, the Father of glory, may give unto you the spirit of wisdom and revelation in the knowledge of him:*
>
> *The eyes of your understanding are being enlightened, so that ye may know what the hope of his calling is and what the riches of the glory of his inheritance are in the saints. And what is the exceeding greatness of his power to us who believe, according to the working of his mighty power?*
>
> *Which he wrought in Christ, when he raised him from the dead and set him at his own right hand in the heavenly places,*
>
> *Far above all principality, power, might, dominion, and every name that is named, not only in this world but also in that which is to come: And hath put all things under his feet and gave him to be the head over all things to the church.*
>
> *Which is his body, the fulness of him that filleth all in all. Ephesians 1:15-23*

This realization is to begin in this age, as spiritual truth is embraced through faith and will continue throughout the years to come. The body of Christ will be His agents, His stewards of God's mysteries, and His ambassadors to this creation's hosts.

Members of His body on earth may die a physical death before He returns, but the unity of the members of His body is so complete that they will be roused together and rise together to meet Him in the air. His body of believing members will be extracted from this earth as a unified body, whether having been put to sleep in death or remaining alive until He comes.

> *For if we believe that Jesus died and rose again, even so, those who sleep in Jesus will God bring with him.*
>
> *For this we say unto you by the word of the Lord, that we which are alive and remain unto the coming of the Lord shall not prevent them which are asleep. For the Lord himself shall descend from heaven with a shout, with the voice of the archangel, and with the trump of God; and the dead in Christ shall rise first:*
>
> *Then we which are alive and remain shall be caught up together with them in the clouds, to meet the Lord in the air, and so shall we ever be with the Lord. I Thessalonians 4:14–17*

When the body of Christ is caught up together to be joined to Him in the clouds, then the total change of their bodies will occur, as Paul described in Philippians, chapter 3.

> *Brethren, be followers together of me, and mark them that walk so as ye have us for an ensample.*
>
> *(For many walk, of whom I have told you often and now tell you even weeping, that they are the enemies of the cross of Christ:*

> *(Whose end is destruction, whose God is their belly, and whose glory is in their shame, who mind earthly things.)*
>
> *For our conversation is in heaven; from whence also we look for the Saviour, the Lord Jesus Christ:*
>
> *Who shall change our vile body, that it may be fashioned like unto his glorious body, according to the working whereby he is able even to subdue all things unto himself? Philippians 3:17-21*

The total change in our outward physical bodies is the result of our identification with the Lord. As He identified with us in His body that was *in the likeness of sinful flesh (Romans 8:3)*, He tasted both sin and death in His crucifixion, being completely joined with us as to His outward body.

The second element of Paul's gospel to the nations focuses on Christ's body. As you recall, the first element focuses on His blood, which results in *justification*. In the death of His Son, He has accomplished total *reconciliation* with humanity.

> *Much more, then, being now justified by his blood, we shall be saved from wrath through him.*
>
> *¹⁰ For if, when we were enemies, we were reconciled to God by the death of his Son, much more, being reconciled, we shall be saved by his life. Romans 5-9-10*

The word for the gift of reconciliation is *katallage (Strong's #2643, an exchange)*. This word represents a total change in the relationship between God and humanity, which was estranged by Adam's disobedience. Humanity, in its old Adamic state, became a disunited multitude of enemies of God. As humans, we all became enemies, not because it was our choice, but due to Adam's defection in the garden.

But now, humanity's relationship with God has totally changed through the death of God's Son. Moreover, this total change will be realized in the manifestation of the sons of God, the Sonship that the Body of Christ awaits. At that moment, we will exchange an old body affected by sin and death for a new body that is both sinless and immortal.

Now, because of the death of God's Son, we are no longer enemies of God, but children within His family. Currently, as children, we are temporarily placed under tutors and governors, expected to leave our minority, and placed in the family as mature sons. In that state of sonship, we represent the Father and His Son to the creation as heirs of God and joint heirs with Christ. There is no greater honor bestowed upon any other creature.

As we remain in the first creation, we are alive in this world in our old bodies from Adam, but now, at the same time, in Christ, we are a new creation; the old has passed away, and all things have become new (II Corinthians 5:17). In our outer bodies, we are with Adam. In our inner man, we are spiritually joined to the New Humanity.

Paul's admonition to the church at Philippi cited above begins with his instructions to follow him as their apostle and walk with the others who have Paul as their example. He uses the joint word for those who follow together, *summimetes (Strong's #G483d, an imitator of others).*

From this, it is clear that believers who have not embraced the clear teachings of Paul may find themselves as opposers of the truths of his gospel. If their resistance increases due to the hostility between the flesh and the spirit, they may even be classified as *enemies of the cross of Christ.* At the cross, the old was put away.

Those who closely follow Paul's teachings and his example of commitment to the gospel are no longer citizens of this world. Their commonwealth of citizenship belongs in the heavenly realm (Philippians 3:20), where Christ resides now, and from where He will depart to come back to earth for His body.

At that time, He will transform our bodies to resemble His glorious body. This will provide evidence to the creation that He is able to *subdue all things unto Himself.*

In the interim, as the body awaits His appearance, we are to exercise ourselves in a ministry that is unique to His body. Based upon the total change that has occurred between the Father and all of humanity, both the sinners and the saints, He has entrusted the body of Christ with a ministry that the church, His body on earth, is to proclaim and teach.

> *For the love of Christ constraineth us, because we thus judge that if one died for all, then we were all dead.*
>
> *And that he died for all, that they which live should not henceforth live unto themselves, but unto him which died for them, and rose again.*
>
> *Wherefore henceforth know we no man after the flesh: yea, though we have known Christ after the flesh, yet now henceforth know we him no more.*
>
> *Therefore, if any man be in Christ, he is a new creature: old things are passed away; behold, all things are made new.*
>
> *And all things are of God, who hath reconciled us to himself by Jesus Christ and hath given to us the ministry of reconciliation;*
>
> *To wit, that God was in Christ, reconciling the world unto himself, not imputing their trespasses unto them, and hath committed unto us the word of reconciliation.*
>
> *Now then we are ambassadors for Christ, as though God did beseech you by us: we pray you in Christ's stead, be ye reconciled to God.*

> *For he hath made him to be sin for us, who knew no sin, that we might be made the righteousness of God in him. II Corinthians 5:14–21*

You may ask, how do you get into Christ? We have previously discussed that God saw His Son, Jesus Christ, as representing all of humanity. When He went to the cross as the Son of Man, He became the *last Adam*. When he was raised from the dead, He became the *second man*.

God put us in Christ, just as we were all in Adam. It is God's doing.

We, as humans, cannot grasp these things with our fleshly minds. But, as spiritual beings, we are to embrace these spiritual matters by faith. When God says it, He wants us to believe it. He provides faith that He will nourish and nurture to grow ever stronger.

The unity of the faith concerning these matters of consequence does not occur simply by acknowledging the truth as Paul proclaims in his gospel.

Faith must result in action. Paul continues beyond the joint truths presented in Romans 6 to proceed past *knowing,* to live with Him unto God.

> *For in that he died, he died unto sin once: but in that he liveth, he liveth unto God.*
>
> *Likewise reckon ye also yourselves to be dead indeed unto sin, but alive unto God through Jesus Christ our Lord.*
>
> *Let not sin therefore reign in your mortal body, that ye should obey it in the lusts thereof.*
>
> *Neither yield ye your members as instruments of unrighteousness unto sin: but yield yourselves unto God, as those that are alive from the dead, and your members as instruments of righteousness unto God.*

> *For sin shall not have dominion over you: for ye are not under the law, but under grace. Romans 6:10-14*

We know that the *blood of Christ* frees us from the penalty of our sins. In Romans 6, we are to also know that *the death of Christ* frees us from the power of sin. Paul has previously explained in the chapter that Christ's death is also the death of the Old Humanity so that we should no longer serve sin in our mortal bodies (Romans 6:6).

It is interesting that Romans is the sixth book in the New Testament; the Old Humanity is first mentioned in the sixth chapter, the sixth verse. Depicted numerically, that is 666.

Since He died unto sin once, He lives now unto God (Romans 6:10). Equally, we died unto sin in Him. Therefore, we are also to live unto God, in Him together, as He is also in us.

> *Now if we are dead with Christ, we believe that we shall also live with him.*
>
> *Knowing that Christ, being raised from the dead, dieth no more, death hath no more dominion over him. Romans 6:8-9*

From His death, we are dead with Him. That being so, we shall also live with Him *(suzao, Strong's #G4800, to live together with one, a new life in union with Christ)*. This is yet another of the *joint* words in Romans, Chapter 6.

The knowledge that you have in your mind must now be expressed in your daily actions. As you identify with Christ, Paul's gospel and teaching are to become your spiritual guides. God's Spirit bears witness to the truth in His Word, the gospel that was entrusted to Paul.

Identifying with Christ, as was the practice of Paul, is a step-by-step process. Let's view the completion of Romans 6 as the next step.

> *What then? Shall we sin because we are not under the law but under grace? God forbid.*
>
> *Know ye not, that to whom ye yield yourselves servants to obey, his servants ye are to whom ye obey, whether of sin unto death or of obedience unto righteousness?*
>
> *But God be thanked that ye were the servants of sin, but ye have obeyed from the heart that form of doctrine that was delivered to you.*
>
> *Being then made free from sin, ye became the servants of righteousness.*
>
> *I speak after the manner of men because of the infirmity of your flesh, for as ye have yielded your members servants to uncleanness and to iniquity unto iniquity; even so now yield your members servants to righteousness unto holiness.*
>
> *For when ye were the servants of sin, ye were free from righteousness.*
>
> *What fruit had ye then in those things whereof ye are now ashamed? For the end of those things is death.*
>
> *But now, being made free from sin and becoming servants of God, ye have your fruit unto holiness and the end of everlasting life.*
>
> *For the wages of sin is death; but the gift of God is eternal life through Jesus Christ, our Lord. Romans 6:15-23*

Freedom from the power and dominion of sin over Old Humanity leads to Christ's victory in equipping the Romans as 12 servants of God. This freedom is the result of being taught by God's spirit to embrace by faith the words of unity contained in the first eight verses of Romans, Chapter 6.

In summary, the words are *sunthapto, sumphutos, sustauroo, and suzao.*

These words may be simplified in English as *buried with, generated with, crucified with, and lived with.*

These joint words are necessary in pursuit of the goal of being recognized as a son of God. Sons of God are led by the Spirit of God (Romans 8:14).

The nullification of the *body of sin* is of specific importance, as mentioned previously. However, the KJV misrepresents the situation by stating that it has been *destroyed*. But such is not the case. Paul uses an important word to illustrate what spiritually has occurred to our *Old Humanity*.

The word is *katargeo (Strong's #G2673, to render entirely idle)*. The rule and reign of sin over the human race have been entirely made idle by the death of God's Son. Sin will remain in charge until each human sees themselves liberated from the power of it by being included in His death.

By faith in the operation of God, sin has no more dominion over Him, nor over the members of humanity that are members of His body in Him. The just shall live by faith, and this is one of the important elements that faith must embrace.

Now, a new consideration comes to light that also requires an element of faith to be applied. Believers are not *under law, but under grace (Romans 6:15)*. Service to God cannot be conducted in the flesh. Paul learned this valuable lesson and wants all members of Christ's body to know the next step in our joint quest to move from spiritual minority to majority. As he reported in Romans, Chapter1, Paul served God in his spirit.

The dominion of sin has come to an end with the death of Christ. *Katargeo* has a new application as Paul continues his discussion of the elements of Christ's saving work in Romans, Chapter 7.

> *Know ye not, brethren, (for I speak to them that know the law), how that the law hath dominion over a man as long as he liveth?*
>
> *For the woman who hath a husband is bound by the law to her husband so long as he liveth; but if the husband is dead, she is loosed from the law of her husband.*
>
> *So then if, while her husband liveth, she is married to another man, she shall be called an adulteress; but if her husband is dead, she is free from that law; so that she is no adulteress, though she is married to another man.*
>
> *Wherefore, my brethren, ye also are dead to the law by the body of Christ; that ye should be married to another, even to him who is raised from the dead, that we should bring forth fruit unto God.*
>
> *For when we were in the flesh, the motions of sins, which were by the law, did work in our members to bring forth fruit unto death.*
>
> *But now we are delivered from the law, that being dead wherein we were held; that we should serve in newness of spirit and not in the oldness of the letter. Romans 7:1-6*

In these verses, Paul speaks of the dominion of the law. As long as a man is alive, he is under the law's jurisdiction. This is illustrated in the marriage relationship. The married woman is under the law of her husband. However, if her husband dies, his law becomes idle (katargeo) to her. She is no longer under the dominion of his law. She has been *loosed (katargeo)* from the law of her husband.

She is not to marry another man while her first husband is alive, but if he dies, she may legally be joined to another. In that case, she would not be considered an adulteress. A woman is not to be under the law of two men at the same time.

We, as His saints, are the subject of Paul's example, where he uses a woman subject to her husband's law. In our case, the husband (the old man) is representative of our human bodies. The law of the husband on a spiritual level is the law of sin and death in our members. Our flesh is like the woman in Paul's example. She cannot bear spiritual fruit for God.

An additional application of the woman being subject to the law of her husband is illustrated in Adam and Eve. Notice that when she ate the first of the forbidden fruits, she did not begin to die. It was when Adam ate that both sin and death entered into both Adam and Eve at the same time (Genesis 3:6-7). The law of the husband, Adam, in the entry of sin and death passed immediately to Eve as she was subject to him, and they were considered one flesh by God.

Since we have also died with Christ, sin's dominion over us has ended. As Paul explains, we are also dead to the law through Christ's body. Being joined to another (Christ), who was raised from the dead, we are now to bring forth fruit to God (Romans 7:4-5) by the power of the law of the New Man in Christ, the law of the spirit of life in Christ Jesus (8:2).

In our former state, being in darkness, our members brought forth fruit unto death. But now, the law no longer holds us captive, as we have been delivered (katargeo) from its power. We can bring forth pleasing fruit to God as we *serve in newness of spirit and not in the oldness of the letter (Romans 7:6b)*.

Paul has previously stated that *If we are dead with Christ we believe that we shall also live with Him (Romans 6:8)*. A more accurate rendering may be stated as *Now if we died together with Christ*. Dying is a continual process leading to the state of death, which is constant until the resurrection.

When did He begin to die?

When He began to shed His blood, He began to pour out His soul. When He agonized in prayer in the garden before He was arrested, His sweat fell like drops of blood.

> *And being in agony he prayed more earnestly; and his sweat was as great as drops of blood falling to the ground. Luke 22:44*

After his mock trial, Pilate sent Jesus to be scourged, causing His blood to freely flow from His body. When the soldiers of the governor placed a platted crown of thorns on His head, He bled some more. He was then led away to be crucified, where Jesus bled out.

And finally, both water and blood were issued from His spear-pierced side (John 19:34).

During all these mocking indignities, His royal blood streamed from His body.

He was pouring out His soul as full payment for the souls of many.

> *Even as the Son of Man came not to be ministered unto, but to minister, and to give his life a ransom for many. Matthew 20:28, and Mark 10:45*

We have discussed in this manuscript how important are both His blood and His body. Here, in this verse, we see that He gave up His soul.

The soul, which contains the mind, will, and emotions, is the essence of the personality and character of each of us. Being comprised of three parts: body, soul, and spirit, each part is vital to our being a living human.

Where is the soul?

Spirit relates to breath. The oxygen we breathe transfers into our physical system the spirit of life. The life-giving oxygen transmits life into our blood, which courses through our physical frame, providing the life-sustaining oxygen to our various parts.

The soul is in the blood. Moses explained this to Israel in Leviticus, Chapter 17.

> *[10] And whatsoever man there be of the house of Israel, or of the strangers that sojourn among you, that eateth any manner of blood; I will even set my face against that soul that eateth blood, and will cut him off from among his people.*
>
> *[11] For the life of the flesh is in the blood: and I have given it to you upon the altar to make an atonement for your souls: for it is the blood that maketh an atonement for the soul.*
>
> *[12] Therefore I said unto the children of Israel, No soul of you shall eat blood, neither shall any stranger that sojourneth among you eat blood. Leviticus 17:10-12*

The life of the flesh that is in the blood is the soul (psuche) of that person.

Remember that in the garden during the creation phase recorded in Genesis, God demonstrated the difference between the spirit, soul, and body of a person.

> *And the Lord God formed man of the dust of the ground and breathed into his nostrils the breath of life; and man became a living soul.*
> *Genesis 2:7*

Adam's body was made of soil. God breathed into Him the breath and spirit of life. When the spirit was united with his body, Adam became a living soul.

Jesus, as to His body, was generated by God in His human mother, Mary, by the Holy Spirit. In her, His body was divinely placed. And, as the two components—spirit and body—were united, He became a living soul.

His uniqueness, as previously discussed, from all other humans who are naturally born from a human father and a human mother, was that He was free from both sin and death. A human father would have passed both of God's enemies on to all his children.

Jesus was dying as His blood continued to pour forth. His soul was the ransom payment for all to receive the gracious gift of forgiveness by faith.

Finally, the last of the blood emptied from His crucified frame as the soldier thrust his sword into His side. His poured-out soul was the full payment for all the sins of the world.

> *The Jews therefore, because it was the preparation that the bodies should not remain upon the cross on the Sabbath day, (for that Sabbath day was a high day), besought Pilate that their legs might be broken and that they might be taken away.*
>
> *Then came the soldiers, and they broke the legs of the first and of the other, which was crucified with him.*
>
> *But when they came to Jesus and saw that he was dead already, they broke not his legs.*

> *But one of the soldiers with a spear pierced his side, and forthwith came there blood and water. John 19:31-34*

The holy, sinless blood had finished the work of atonement for the sins of the whole world, just as John the Baptist foresaw at the Jordan River when Jesus, the Lamb of God, came to be baptized (John 3:13 –17).

The narrative of His sentence of death ended with His crucifixion. The four gospels—Matthew, Mark, Luke, and John—graphically depict the death of Christ Jesus, the Son of God, and as the Son of man. He accomplished all the things the Father sent Him to finish.

The Jewish believers believed that He would restore the kingdom to Israel. What they did not perceive at the time of the fulfillment of His first mission, was that He came not just for them, but for the entire race of humanity. His victory over His enemies was spiritual.

The apostle Paul expanded the mystery of His mission in detail through his letters. Paul explained that the Lord's universal saving work applies to the nullification of the Old Humanity in Him, followed by the creation and resurrection of the New Humanity.

The realization of this mission is universal. In His death, the old is passed away. In His life, the new has come forth.

The common faith pertaining to the forgiveness of sins by Christ's shed blood is shared by all who believe. The power of God's merciful justification renders each believing person covered over by His grace.

The joint faith pertaining to the crucifixion, death, and burial of God's Son pertains to all of humanity as well. When He was raised from the dead, the justification was finalized for each person who had faith in themselves. If He wasn't raised, saving faith is void.

The application of joint faith is realized in the *sun* words that we are studying in this manuscript as one of the chief purposes of the unity between the Father, the Son, and the New Humanity created in Christ.

We are heeding Paul's words of instruction so that we may arrive, as a body, into a realm of true unity in anticipation of the Lord's return. This admonition is found in Ephesians.

> *I therefore, the prisoner of the Lord, beseech you that ye walk worthy of the vocation wherewith ye are called, with all lowliness and meekness, with long suffering, forbearing one another in love; Endeavoring to keep the unity of the Spirit in the bond of peace. Ephesians 4:1-3*

As we begin to understand the adversary's chief aim in turning mankind away from God, it is realized that he has always sought to be worshipped. Throughout the ages, beginning with the deception in the garden, the master of dishonest trickery has transformed himself and his minions into angels of righteousness.

If humanity is enthralled by maintaining an outward form of worshipping God through rituals and false idols, the religious fraud will continue unabated. In these last days, God will turn humanity over to a strong delusion that will prepare the nations for the ultimate deceiver, the man of sin. When working throughout the prior centuries in a hidden manner, the son of perdition will openly use his greatest deceptive strategies to gain the ultimate worship of the deceived masses to a final crescendo.

Then, the Master of Truth will descend from His heavenly throne to end the charade of the counterfeit system of religion with His mighty power, exposing the sham of the adversary's desire to be worshipped.

There is only one who is worthy of all glory, honor, and praise from His Father, as He is supremely pleased with His Son's sacrifice motivated by divine truth and love.

CHAPTER 5

THE GLORIOUS LIBERTY OF THE CHILDREN OF GOD

UNITY IN CHRIST

> *For the earnest expectation of the creature waiteth for the manifestation of the sons of God.*
>
> *For the creature was made subject to vanity, not willingly, but by reason of him who hath subjected the same in hope,*
>
> *Because the creature itself will also be delivered from the bondage of corruption into the glorious liberty of the children of God. Romans 8:19-21*

There is ultimate freedom in the unity that is in Christ Jesus. God, the Father, has gloriously changed humanity through His Son's saving work. This total change in the new humanity replaces the divisions of the old with the unification of the new.

Likewise, this current creation will be subject to a dramatic change as well. At present, creation is in a state of uselessness with no apparent purpose beyond displaying God's power and order. This is the meaning of *vanity*. If sin, death, and corruption exist, the purpose of them all is in question.

But, at the same time, creation is subject to *hope*. Both the current state of vanity *and hope* are God's doing. The expectation arises from the intention of God to release creation from the condition of slavery to corruption that causes perishing from decay.

This creation will change when Jesus returns to claim those who are His. Israel will be liberated to fulfill its calling on earth. The body of Christ will be ever-present with Him wherever He may be, on earth or functioning in heavenly places.

Reborn Israel, God's nation Son, will glorify Him on earth. His glory will also be displayed in the sons joined to Christ as His body.

The son placing *(huiosthesia)* will produce this glorious splendor.

The overpowering unity that was first expressed between the Father and His Son will be expressed in the body of Christ as the first fruits of the spirit (Romans 8:23). The unity of the spirit will pour forth from the depths of God's love, which is to be mutually expressed in Christ's body before the Son of Man returns.

Paul clearly exhorted the church at Ephesus on this vital matter.

> *I therefore, the prisoner of the Lord, beseech you that ye walk worthy of the vocation wherewith ye are called,*
>
> *With all lowliness and meekness, with long suffering, forbearing one another in love;*
>
> *Endeavoring to keep the unity of the Spirit in the bond of peace. Ephesians 4:1-3*

Love never fails, as Paul proclaims in I Corinthians 13.

The believing members of the body learn that the dominion of sin expressed through the Old Humanity has been put to an end by being crucified with Christ. The old humanity was in Him in His death.

Faith apprehends the truth that, after being baptized into His death, all were placed in the tomb with Him. Being unified with Christ's body in His crucifixion, death, and burial has thoroughly exempted the unified believer from the demands of the law, as the flesh is not subjected to its mandates.

This life of freedom defines the sons of God as their inclusion in the former events of His death prevails in His new life, His resurrection.

> *For as many as are led by the Spirit of God, they are the sons of God. Romans 8:14*

Members of His body realize freedom from slavery, both from sin and death, through the full proclamation of Paul's gospel commending the victorious sacrifice of the Son of Man. The liberty of His saving work is magnified in the joint realization with other members who embrace the unifying truths of Paul's gospel.

As the joint members maintain the unity of the spirit, they grasp the unity of the faith that comes from the leadership in the body who embrace Paul's gospel. They are called by God for the preparation of the saints, the body being edified and matured through their service of proclamation.

> *And he gave some, apostles; and some, prophets; and some, evangelists; and some, pastors and teachers;*
>
> *For the perfecting of the saints, for the work of the ministry, for the edifying of the body of Christ:*

> *Till we all come in the unity of the faith, and of the knowledge of the Son of God, unto a perfect man, unto the measure of the stature of the fulness of Christ: Ephesians 4:11–13*

When functioning together in Paul's gospel, one plants the seeds of Paul's gospel while another waters (I Corinthians 3:6). God then causes spiritual growth in others, who will in turn begin to function in their calling as directed by the Spirit.

The glorious liberty of the children of God will be amplified as the creation itself is joined to the final course of work in this splendid child birthing process.

> *For we know that the whole creation groaneth and travaileth in pain together until now. Romans 8:22*

We are persuaded that this wondrous suffering will lead to the pure joy of deliverance. Groaning in this manner is *sustenazo*, (Strong's #G4959, *to moan jointly, to groan together*). Travailing in pain together is *sunodino*, (Strong's #G4944, *to have birthing pangs in company with, simultaneously, in expectation of relief from suffering.*)

Paul received these marvelous revelations of the spirit during his later service as a prisoner of the Lord. While held captive, his separation from the outside Gentile world of Rome provided the perfect isolated environment for the freedom to be expressed in the spiritual words of his prison letters. The overwhelming need for unity in the body was conveyed to him by the spirit of Christ.

Paul realized that the spiritual forces of the kingdom of darkness would suppress the edification of the body far into the future, to the time of reigning grace. The maturity of the body would become of primary importance for spiritual adulthood, made possible by Paul's gospel proclaimed in the church.

> *That we henceforth be no more children, tossed to and from, and carried about with every wind of doctrine, by the sleight of men, and cunning craftiness, whereby they lie in wait to deceive;*
>
> *But speaking the truth in love may grow up into him in all things, which is the head, even Christ:*
>
> *From whom the whole body fitly joined together and compacted by that which every joint supplieth, according to the effectual working in the measure of every part, maketh increase of the body unto the edifying of itself in love. Ephesians 4:14-16*

The joint body will become *fitly joined together (sunarmologeo, Strong's #G4883, organized completely)* and *compacted by that which every joint supplieth (sumbibazo, Strong's #G4822, to cause to coalesce, to make or fit together in affection)*.

Every member of the joint body will operate efficiently and effectively in accordance with God's gifts and energy. Vigorous growth will originate and freely flow from the love of God.

The realization of ultimate freedom resulting from the coming of the Lord in His wondrous glory will be apparent throughout the entire creation. The awe of Christ's crowning victory will be on display as the body of Christ is revealed in a magnificent celestial display.

As this concluding era is approaching, the body of Christ, in addition to the growth in knowledge and faith, will exult in the Godly expression of the grace of hope, which must come forth in the ever-increasing expectation of the redemption of our body (Romans 8:23).

> *For we are saved by hope, but hope that is seen is not hope; for what a man seeth, why doth he yet hope for?*
>
> *For we are saved by hope, but hope that is seen is not hope; for what a man seeth, why doth he yet hope for? But if we hope for that we see not, then do we with patience wait for it. Romans 8:24-25*

The fullness of our salvation will be accomplished. Faith has looked back upon all that our loving Father, through Jesus Christ, His Son, has accomplished in bringing to fruition the holy plan of salvation. Now, we are to look forward in expectation to that which the creation yearns to realize concerning God's boundless love.

Faith and hope will coalesce into a joyful expectation of His arrival.

We are to anticipate with pleasure, joyfully, and confidently that which Paul has written to the churches and to his loyal fellow workers.

He closes this section of his Romans letter to commend to the body the ever-present Spirit for unifying with the Father and the Son and completing this royal mission.

> *Likewise, the Spirit also helpeth our infirmities, for we know not what we should pray for as we ought, but the Spirit itself maketh intercession for us with groanings that cannot be uttered.*
>
> *And he that searcheth the hearts knoweth what the mind of the Spirit is, because he maketh intercession for the saints according to the will of God. Romans 8:26-27*

The Spirit of God is the imperceptible power of God to bring into existence all things divinely provided to meet the spiritual sustenance that the body needs. God reveals those things, of which we are too weak in the flesh to even be aware, to the Spirit so that we can be helped by the intercession on our behalf.

God knows our hearts, and the Spirit knows the heart of God. The Spirit brings us into even greater unity by pleading for the saints in accord with God.

Here we find the final *sun* words, words of unity, in the eighth chapter of Paul's Romans letter.

> *And we know that all things work together for good to those who love God, to those who are called according to his purpose. Romans 8:28*

What a marvelous testimony. If we kept this daily in mind, we would see things working together as our Lord sees them.

All things work together for good. The spiritual eyesight that Paul described surely filled the heart and mind of Christ. It is to be a focus of our minds as well. Working together is another *sun* word. It is characteristic of the unity between the Father and the Son. It must also be the key word between all members of Christ's body.

Working together is *sunergeo, (Strong's #G4903, to be a fellow worker, to put forth power together and thereby assist).*

When believers are divided, especially by the doctrines of their separate beliefs, they cannot work together in unity. Or their religious traditions may place barriers that separate them from others who may not follow the same path. They become divided, much like the Pharisees of Jesus' day.

Paul was plainly speaking about this. He abhorred divisions in the body. In his first letter to the church at Corinth, in the very opening remarks, He rebuked them for their prejudicial sects (I Corinthians 1:12-13).

Paul's advice to the church at Philippi applies to all who choose to follow his spiritual guidance.

> *Finally, brethren, whatsoever things are true, whatsoever things are honest, whatsoever things are just, whatsoever things are pure, whatsoever things are lovely, whatsoever things are of good report; if there be any virtue, and if there be any praise, think on these things.*
>
> *Those things, which ye have both learned, received, heard, and seen in me, do: and the God of peace shall be with you. Philippians 4:8-9*

If our testimony mirrored that which Paul states above, unity would be unbroken.

Separation from God, where sin and unbelief abound, would disappear.

> *Who shall separate us from the love of Christ? shall tribulation, or distress, or persecution, or famine, or nakedness, or peril, or sword?*
>
> *As it is written, for thy sake, we are killed all day long; we are accounted as sheep for the slaughter. Romans 8:35-36*

God works all things together for good for those who are called by God according to His purpose. The man of the flesh views these trials as evil working for a destructive purpose. That, however, is emphatically not true. These trials are allowed to enter the lives of believers, coming from God's love to cleanse and purify.

Since we are sheep following the shepherd, our service to God is of a sacrificial nature. Isaiah's prophecy of the Lord in this regard is meant for the members of His body, along with the chosen of Israel, as a type of life of service that pleases the Father.

> *He was oppressed, and he was afflicted, yet he opened not his mouth. He is brought as a lamb to the slaughter, and as a sheep before her shearers is dumb, so he openeth not his mouth. Isaiah 53:7*

Jeremiah referred to himself in like manner.

> *But I was like a lamb or an ox that is brought to the slaughter, and I knew not that they had devised devices against me, saying, Let us destroy the tree with the fruit thereof, and let us cut him off from the land of the living, that his name may be no more remembered. Jeremiah 11:19*

The unity of His body on earth, characterized by both the unity of the spirit and the unity of the faith, will provide a catalyst for the unity of the tribes of Israel that come through their time of great tribulation. The nation of Israel will be integrated into the saving work of our Lord.

Their renewal, brought forth from the new covenant that God will cut with them, will enable them to fulfill their calling that has been in abeyance since Malachi's prophecy.

Their restoration will be affected by a purifying, fiery trial that will result in such far-reaching unity that it will project them into their calling of the unification of the nations. As they reunite with God through much trial and tribulation, their guidance and example will prove that Jesus came to restore all things in the new creation.

This incredible work through God's chosen nation on earth has been foretold through the prophets and holy men in scripture. Israel will be unified in that purpose, as Jeremiah once envisioned.

> *The Lord spoke to Jeremiah, saying: Thus, speaketh the Lord God of Israel, saying; Write thee all the words that I have spoken unto thee in a book.*
>
> *For, lo, the days come, saith the Lord, that I will bring again the captivity of my people Israel and Judah, saith the Lord: and I will cause them to return to the land that I gave to their fathers, and they shall possess it.*
>
> *And these are the words that the Lord spoke concerning Israel and concerning Judah.*
>
> *For thus saith the Lord: We have heard a voice of trembling, of fear, and not of peace.*
>
> *Ask ye now, and see whether a man doth travail with child? wherefore do I see every man with his hands on his loins, as a woman in travail, and all faces are turned into paleness?*
>
> *Alas! for that day is great, so that none is like it: it is even the time of Jacob's trouble, but he shall be saved out of it. Jeremiah 30:1-7*

Here, in a single expression, *Jacob's trouble,* the Lord is describing the considerably difficult times that await the chosen nation to prepare them for their spiritual service. The balance of the verses, however, brings hope that the captivity of the people will again be reversed, and they will once again possess their inheritance and fulfill their divine calling on earth.

Jeremiah foretells of the cutting of a new covenant with His reunited people.

> *Behold, the days come, saith the Lord, that I will make a new covenant with the house of Israel and with the house of Judah. Jeremiah 31:31*

This promise of a future covenant, a new covenant, joining them again into the commonwealth of Israel, is attested to by the writer of Hebrews.

> *For finding fault with them, he saith, Behold, the days come, saith the Lord, when I will make a new covenant with the house of Israel and with the house of Judah: Hebrews 8:8*

As the promised restoration cited in both Jeremiah 31:31 and Hebrews 8:8 specifies, God will put His law into their minds and write it in their hearts.

The promise of the law written in their hearts is further expanded in Ezekiel, chapter 36.

> *A new heart also will I give you, and a new spirit will I put within you; and I will take away the stony heart out of your flesh, and I will give you a heart of flesh. Ezekiel 36:26*

In the restoration that the disciples of Christ longed to see, the making of the new covenant with the reunited houses of Israel, with both a new heart and a new spirit, will equip the nation for the service of God anew.

> *For it shall come to pass in that day, saith the Lord of hosts, that I will break his yoke from off thy neck and will burst thy bonds, and strangers shall no longer serve themselves of him:*
>
> *But they shall serve the Lord their God, and David their king, whom I will raise up unto them.*
>
> *Therefore, fear thou not, O my servant Jacob, saith the Lord; neither be dismayed, O Israel: for, lo, I will save thee from afar, and thy seed from the land of their captivity; and Jacob shall return, and shall be in rest, and be quiet, and none shall make him afraid. Jeremiah 30:8-10*

And the Lord further expands His sure promises in Jeremiah, Chapter 32.

And now therefore thus saith the Lord, the God of Israel, concerning this city, whereof ye say, it shall be delivered into the hand of the king of Babylon by the sword, by the famine, and by the pestilence;

Behold, I will gather them out of all countries, whether I have driven them in my anger, in my fury, and in great wrath; and I will bring them again unto this place, and I will cause them to dwell safely.

And they shall be my people, and I will be their God.

And I will give them one heart and one way that they may fear me forever, for the good of them, and of their children after them:

And I will make an everlasting covenant with them, that I will not turn away from them to do them good; but I will put my fear in their hearts, that they shall not depart from me.

Yea, I will rejoice over them to do them good, and I will plant them in this land assuredly with my whole heart and with my whole soul.

For thus saith the Lord: Like as I have brought all this great evil upon these people, so will I bring upon them all the good that I have promised them.

And fields shall be bought in this land, whereof ye say. It is desolate without man or beast; it is given into the hand of the Chaldeans.

Men shall buy fields for money, subscribe evidences, seal them, and take witnesses in the land of Benjamin, and in the places about Jerusalem, and in the cities of Judah, and in the cities of the mountains, and in the cities of the valley, and in the cities of the south; for I will cause their captivity to return, saith the Lord. Jeremiah 32:36-44

Jesus Christ, as the suffering servant, came in His first advent as a minister to the circumcision to confirm the promises granted to the fathers (Romans 15:8).

So that Israel may yet identify with their Messiah, who, as the Son of Man, previously came to suffer and die, they are ordained of God to pass through the great fire of tribulation. Even though their history is replete with trials and judgments, *Jacob's trouble* will far surpass their past suffering. The greatest trial is yet to come for Jacob's family.

Jesus identified fully with Israel in the short term of His ministry. In so doing, He confirmed the promises given to their fathers, as Paul reported: promises of restoration and reconciliation.

> *Now I say that Jesus Christ was a minister of the circumcision for the truth of God, to confirm the promises made unto the fathers: Romans 15:8*

The restoration of Israel is imminent. The inner change within their hearts will launch them forth into the world of nations that have so long reproached and persecuted them. They will overcome the evil of prejudice with good springing from the love of God poured into their hearts.

Paul, the apostle to the nations, was provided with a unique spiritual vantage point concerning Israel and the nations. He was, in times past, a fierce opponent of the early church. In his prior life, before his conversion, Paul was the epitome of Jewish religious zeal. He was thoroughly taught all necessary knowledge of the oracles of God and of the tradition of the fathers that he would need as a high-ranking Pharisee.

When he was confronted with a blinding revelation of Jesus on the road to Damascus (Acts 9:1-9), he was totally changed, regaining not only his physical sight but also unique spiritual insight into the purposes and plans of God. He was blessed with a special calling for the nations.

Being commissioned by Jesus as the apostle to the nations, he was able to interpret the meaning of Jesus' ministry in a new light. He was given revelations concerning Israel, the nations, and the body of Christ that clarified God's wondrous plan of salvation. He was fully qualified to speak of Israel's temporary spiritual blindness that would be reversed at the proper time when God finalized the plans for the Gentiles to come to Him through the church. The next phase will be Israel's ministry.

In Chapter 11 of his letter to the Romans, Paul provides his exclusive insight into the future renewal of Israel, illuminating the role of the Gentile believers in their restoration as this current era draws to a close.

He emphasizes that Israel's fall brings forth benefits for creation. These blessings will belong to them because of their miraculous recovery. However, during this time, they must endure fiery trials that will lead to their thorough cleansing.

Here is part of his report.

> *I say then, Hath God cast away his people? God forbid. For I am also an Israelite, of the seed of Abraham, of the tribe of Benjamin.*
>
> *God hath not cast away his people, which he foreknew. Wot ye not what the scripture saith of Elias? how he maketh intercession to God against Israel, saying,*
>
> *Lord, they have killed thy prophets and digged down thine altars; and I am left alone, and they seek my life.*
>
> *But what saith the answer of God unto him? I have reserved to myself seven thousand men, who have not bowed the knee to the image of Baal.*
>
> *Even so then at this present time also there is a remnant according to the election of grace.*

> *And if by grace, then is it no more of works: otherwise, grace is no more grace. But if it be of works, then it is no more grace: otherwise, work is no more work.*
>
> *What then? Israel hath not obtained that which he seeketh for; but the election hath obtained it, and the rest were blinded.*
>
> *(According as it is written, God hath given them the spirit of slumber, eyes that they should not see, and ears that they should not hear) to this day. Romans 11:1-8*

There is a remnant of believing Israelites to this day. The rest remain blinded to the gospel until their sight is restored. Israel's temporary fall has resulted in magnanimous benefits to creation, especially to the Gentile nations, which are partially saved in this current phase but will be led by God in the future to those by whom they were mercilessly persecuted.

> *Now if the fall of them be the riches of the world and the diminishing of them the riches of the Gentiles, how much more their fulness? Romans 11:12*

And what may these riches be? Is there actually great good that has resulted in the discomfiture of the holy nation?

Paul continues.

> *For if the casting away of them be the reconciling of the world, what shall the receiving of them be but life from the dead? Romans 11:15*

Israel's casting away will be followed in God's time by the *receiving of them from the dead.*

Does Paul advise the believers as to when that will occur?

> *For I would not, brethren, that ye should be ignorant of this mystery, lest ye should be wise in your own conceits; that blindness in part happened to Israel, until the fulness of the Gentiles came in. Romans 11:25*

God does not abandon, nor forsake the ones He calls and loves.

> *And so all Israel shall be saved; as it is written, there shall come out of Sion the Deliverer, and he shall turn away ungodliness from Jacob.*
>
> *For this is my covenant unto them, when I shall take away their sins.*
>
> *As concerning the gospel, they are enemies for your sakes, but as touching the election, they are beloved for the father's sakes.*
>
> *For the gifts and calling of God are without repentance. Romans 11:26-29*

Israel, as a nation, along with individual Israelite citizens, will identify fully with Him in this critical time as this age draws to a close and the next age begins. The impending momentous events will provide a stage upon which Israel will suffer and survive their most fiery trial, then reign on earth, drawing the nations to God. David's royal line will be brought forth in Christ, for it is written in three witnesses;

> *And in mercy shall the throne be established, and he shall sit upon it in truth in the tabernacle of David, judging, seeking judgment, and hasting righteousness. Isaiah 16:5*

And,

> *And in that day will I raise up the tabernacle of David that is fallen and close up the breaches thereof; and I will raise up his ruins, and I will build it as in the days of old: Amos 9:11*

And,

> *After this, I will return and build again the tabernacle of David, which has fallen down, and I will build again the ruins thereof, and I will set it up. Acts 15:16*

Israel has surely suffered through the ages. At first blush, we may say, from the perspective of the flesh, that they deserved everything they experienced. After all, didn't they crucify God's Son, their Messiah? But that is a short-sighted view. Without doubt, they are an example to all nations that God, the holy One, is rightfully justified and disposed to bring judgment upon evil. But do people understand that He has a rule of operation for the Jew first?

They not only saw Him first, but they also rejected Him first. Because of their scorn for Him, the gospel was presented to the Gentiles.

Before Israel reaches out to the nations with mercy and forgiveness, they must be the first nation to receive mercy in abundance. Paul intimates that such mercy is to come from the body of Christ, which is indebted to Israel for their rejection.

The casting away of Israel is not permanent. Their blindness and stubborn hearts have driven them away from their God. The absolute truth of their return was insisted upon by Paul, as he was *an Israelite, of the seed of Abraham, of the tribe of Benjamin (Romans 11:1b)*. They are God's people on earth whom He foreknows as he quoted the ancient statement of Elijah, the prophet, when he felt that all of Israel had left God except for himself.

God's answer was emphatic. He had reserved unto Himself a remnant that had not bowed the knee to Baal (Romans 11:2 –5).

Israel has not descended to a lower place in the plan of God concerning the kingdom on earth. Their offense to God has resulted in the salvation of the Gentiles, to whom Paul was placed as the apostle to the nations. Their offence has resulted in riches for the creation and the temporary diminishing of their riches to the Gentiles.

God turns evil into good, revealing the depths of His vast love. Paul asks the obvious question: "How much more is their fulness?"

The casting away of Israel has resulted in vast blessings. Not only has the gospel been provided to the Gentiles, but the entire universe benefits in that it has resulted in a total change (katallage) of the cosmos. The vanity to which creation is subject has now been reversed by the casting away of Israel.

This overwhelming fact is a universal change that can be compared to the total change in the relationship with God and humanity accomplished by the death of God's Son, Jesus Christ. The casting away of the nation of Israel, God's nation Son, has totally changed the universe. Is it any wonder that when they are restored, it will be as if they have been raised from the dead? Jesus was resurrected, and so will Israel.

God's judgement is righteously decreed, and the ones being judged acknowledge the justice so rendered as proper and appropriate. The mercy of God has no limit. Righteousness is shared with the one who sees that the judgement is both fair and proper and the penalty is appropriate when dispensed by God. The ones being judged acknowledge that they are unjust, and in like manner of the faith of Abraham, believe in the God that justifies the ungodly being reckoned as righteous (Romans 4:5).

Israel, as a nation, is ordained to perceive God's revelation of His righteousness. Under the law of Moses, they sought after the law of righteousness (Romans 10:3), attempting to justify themselves. At that time, they sought to earn it through their observance of His law. They, as is true of all people, must see that they deserved the penalty for their sins, offenses, and trespasses, but someone far greater than they paid for it. The one who has paid is God, by sending His Son, in the likeness of sin, to condemn sin in the flesh, as Paul reported in Romans 8:3.

John, in his revelation, described the event of His return to the earth, when the kingdom will be restored to Israel.

> *Behold, he cometh with clouds; and every eye shall see him, and they also which pierced him; and all kindreds of the earth shall wail because of him. Even so, Amen. Revelation 1:7*

Jesus came to pay the ransom price to buy back all of Adam's family. He is the kinsman redeemer, as depicted in the Old Testament book of Ruth.

> *Then went Boaz up to the gate and sat him down there; and, behold, the kinsman of whom Boaz spoke came by, unto whom he said, Ho, such a one! Turn aside and sit down here. And he turned aside and sat down.*
>
> *And he took ten men of the elders of the city and said, Sit ye down here. And they sat down.*
>
> *And he said unto the kinsman, Naomi, that is, come again out of the country of Moab, selleth a parcel of land, which was our brother Elimelech's:*
>
> *And I thought to advertise it, saying, Buy it before the inhabitants and before the elders of my people. If thou wilt redeem it, redeem it; but if thou wilt not redeem it, then tell me, that I may know, for there is none to redeem it beside thee, and I am after thee. And he said, I will redeem it.*

Then said Boaz, what day thou buyest the field of the hand of Naomi, thou must buy it also of Ruth the Moabitess, the wife of the dead, to raise up the name of the dead upon his inheritance.

And the kinsman said, I cannot redeem it for myself, lest I mar my own inheritance; redeem thou my right to thyself: for I cannot redeem it.

Now this was the manner in former times in Israel concerning redeeming and concerning changing, for to confirm all things, a man plucked off his shoe and gave it to his neighbor: and this was a testimony in Israel.

Therefore, the kinsman said to Boaz, Buy it for thee. So, he drew off his shoe.

And Boaz said unto the elders, and unto all the people, Ye are witnesses this day, that I have bought all that was Elimelech's, and all that was Chilion's and Mahlon's, from the hand of Naomi.

Moreover, Ruth the Moabitess, the wife of Mahlon, have I purchased to be my wife, to raise up the name of the dead upon his inheritance, that the name of the dead be not cut off from among his brethren and from the gate of his place: ye are witnesses this day. Ruth 4:1-10

We know that through Ruth and Boaz, the line of David, the King, was established. Ruth was an honorable and virtuous Moabite Gentile who joined herself with her mother-in-law, Naomi. When Boaz joined himself to her, they secured together a vital link in the genealogy of our Lord, Jesus.

A major goal of God is for the body of Christ to express the unity that the Father and Son have obtained together. Boaz, in the story of Ruth, expressed the true unity of the family as he came forward to bring her into his family to raise up children, as was required under the law of redemption, so that the family name could be extended.

Jesus Christ, as the kinsman redeemer, has redeemed all of humanity by claiming His rightful duty to the family of God. Ruth, coming from a foreign land, had no claim to the fortunes of the family of God in Israel. After her husband, who was an Israelite, died, Ruth was brought to Boaz, who stepped up for her when the first kinsman redeemer in line withdrew.

The sons of God will manifest the glory of God, with Christ as the head of the body, expressing their collective liberty. Then, freedom will extend within the first creation on behalf of a release from the *bondage of corruption*.

God, the Father, views Israel, the nation, as His son. This is confirmed through Hosea, the prophet.

> *When Israel was a child, then I loved him and called my son out of Egypt. Hosea 11:1*

Matthew, in his gospel, applied Hosea's prophecy statement concerning Israel to Jesus. Joseph had taken Mary, along with their infant Son, Jesus, to Egypt to protect him from Herod's vengeful scheme to kill all the newborn male babies in Bethlehem.

> *And was there until the death of Herod: that it might be fulfilled, which was spoken of the Lord by the prophet, saying, Out of Egypt have I called my son. Matthew 2:15*

As we have previously expressed, Christ Jesus, in His saving work, has secured a release for the body of Christ from the penalty of each believer's sins, including a release from the power of sin because of His sacrificial death on the cross. Both powerful truths are received through faith.

The body of Christ, the church in this era, is the first group, or company, to receive these truths that apply to all humanity. In God's time, according to His plan for the ages, all will see these wondrous truths and will be redeemed.

The Old Humanity was nullified by His death as the *last Adam (I Corinthians 15:45)*. The New Humanity came into existence in Him by His resurrection from the dead as *the second man (I Corinthians 15:47)*.

His saving work has also brought forth an overthrow of death's rule by the nullification of the law of sin and death in the bodies of the members of the Old Humanity. Now, Paul makes it evident that Christ's victory has extended into creation.

In the same manner that humanity has suffered under the rule of sin and death, creation is also suffering from a state of decay. It is subject to the ruin that was introduced through Adam's disobedience. The creation is suffering from a condition of corruption that, if not abated or eliminated by God, will ultimately result in the total degeneration of the first creation.

But God as Creator, the Father of us all, has made provision in Christ that when the body of Christ is revealed, having a total change evidenced by their new bodies, there will be a release of the state of corruption that produces vanity, which is transientness. This is the *earnest expectation of the creation*.

By virtue of their new bodies, the members of Christ's body will be immortal, enjoying freedom from the presence of sin. In their free state, the law of the spirit of life in Christ Jesus will find full expression, uniting the first company of the New Humanity into a cohesive image of God's love, which, in time, will extend to all.

God's son, Israel, as a nation, will be liberated by receiving the provisions of the new covenant that will be given to the nation, reuniting both houses once separated after the death of Solomon. The citizens of Israel will receive new hearts along with God's law being written in their minds. They will represent the Father, as God's son, to the nations.

The royal government of Israel will be ruled by their king, the Lord Jesus Christ. Their priesthood, of the order of Melchezedek, will be overseen by the Lord Jesus as the High Priest (Hebrews 4:14–15). The full expression of the divine priestly service being conducted by Jesus, now in the heavenlies, is described in Hebrews 11:1–11.

> *For every high priest taken from among men is ordained for men in things pertaining to God, so that he may offer both gifts and sacrifices for sins:*
>
> *Who can have compassion on the ignorant and on those who are out of the way? For that, he himself is compassed with infirmity. And by reason hereof he ought, as for the people, so also for himself, to offer for sins.*
>
> *And no man taketh this honour unto himself, but he that is called of God, as was Aaron.*
>
> *So also, Christ glorified not himself to be made a high priest, but he that said unto him: Thou art my Son, today have I begotten thee.*
>
> *As he saith also in another place, Thou art a priest for ever after the order of Melchisedec.*
>
> *Who in the days of his flesh, when he had offered up prayers and supplications with strong crying and tears unto him, was able to save him from death and was heard in that he feared?*
>
> *Though he were a Son, he learned obedience from the things for which he suffered. And being made perfect, he became the author of eternal salvation for all who obeyed him.*
>
> *Called of God a high priest after the order of Melchisedec.*
>
> *Of whom we have many things to say and are hard to utter, seeing ye are dull of hearing.*

Jesus, as the suffering servant, brought to completion the mission to which He was called. As concerning Israel, He ended the Levitical priesthood by the sacrifice of himself. He inaugurated the order of Melchisedec that was foreshadowed in the King of Salem, the King of righteousness, who met Abraham after saving Lot and his family from servitude by the slaughter of the Kings (Genesis 14:1 –20).

Israel, the nation, is God's Son. Christ Jesus is God's beloved Son. The Body of Christ is comprised of many sons of God.

Each will partake in a *son-placing*. Jesus is first, then the body of Christ, and Israel, as a nation, with be elevated to a higher position of authority, power, and responsibility.

God places His Only Begotten Son, and His many sons as He wants recognition of His vast family to join Him in the reconciliation of all things. His sons will praise Him and bring Him glory as they take their assigned positions of responsibility in the kingdom, both on earth and in the heavenlies.

Until the *huiosthesia* (son placing) occurs at the manifestation of the sons of God, service to God by the church on earth is to be characterized by the two unities of Ephesians, Chapter 4, verses 3 and 13.

> *Endeavoring to keep the unity of the Spirit in the bond of peace (vs. 3).*

And,

> *Till we all come in the unity of the faith and of the knowledge of the Son of God, unto a perfect man, unto the measure of the stature of the fulness of Christ (verse 13).*

Unity is a word in Greek, *henotes (Strong's #G1775)*, which describes unanimity or agreement. It comes from a root word, *heis (Strong's #G1520)*, the word for the numeral one.

The unity of the spirit can be expressed as *the oneness of the spirit*. Every believer has the spirit of God residing in their heart. The spirit making its home in the believer can also be referred to as *the spirit of Christ*, in that one of the functions of the spirit of God is to magnify Christ.

The loving characteristics of Christ are to be on full display in His body.

The spirit within the heart develops a disposition that aligns with Christ. It agrees with God and resists the inclinations of flesh, as the spirit and the flesh are at odds with each other (Romans 8:5).

In Christ, the believer's mind is being conditioned by the Spirit to live a life in peace and harmony with others. This spiritual attitude is heightened when two or more believers gather together.

One of Paul's most vocal corrections was directed towards the church at Corinth. He reproved them for demonstrating divisions within the church. The sects of division arose because they were individually choosing certain leaders rather than Christ Jesus, the head of the body.

Divisions within the body are not to be tolerated. As Paul asked, *"Is the body of Christ divided?" (I Corinthians 1:13)*. The word for divided is *merizo*, *(Strong's #G3307)* meaning *to apportion or divide*.

The division was caused by a deeper problem. They were not believing or saying the same things. In a prior verse to I Corinthians 1:13, Paul clearly states the cause. There is a root source for all division in the body of Christ.

> *Now I beseech you, brethren, by the name of our Lord Jesus Christ, that ye all speak the same thing and that there be no divisions among you; but that ye be perfectly joined together in the same mind and in the same judgment. I Corinthians 1:10*

They were to be saying the same thing, having been attuned to the same mind and in the same opinion. They had exaggerated the importance of one specific ritual. It seems that not only were they turning towards certain individuals to follow, but they were even being subjected to baptism in that person's name.

> *Now this I say, that every one of you saith, I am of Paul; and I am of Apollos; and I am of Cephas; and I am of Christ.*
>
> *Is Christ divided? Was Paul crucified for you? Or were ye baptized in the name of Paul?*
>
> *I thank God that I baptized none of you but Crispus and Gaius, Lest anyone say that I had baptized in my own name.*
>
> *And I also baptized the household of Stephanas; besides I do not know whether I baptized any others.*
>
> *For Christ sent me not to baptize but to preach the gospel, not with wisdom of words, lest the cross of Christ be made of no effect. I Corinthians 1:12–17*

The significance of Paul's correction cannot be overstated. The body of Christ, above all things, is to be a unified body without divisions and sects.

And yet, what do we observe in the common church assembly of this age?

This problem of division began immediately in the first century of the history of the church. It continues unabated.

There are numerous reasons for this certain failure of division that Paul expresses in his corrective letter. The underlying cause can be traced to the concluding verse of the section of the letter above.

> *For Christ sent me not to baptize but to preach the gospel, not with wisdom of words, lest the cross of Christ should be made of none effect (verse 17).*

The ritual of water baptism has divided the church from Paul's day to the present. He baptized. This cannot be denied. But he realized later that water baptism obscures the dominant truth of Paul's gospel.

The *cross of Christ* is the focal point of the saving work of Jesus Christ.

The church at Corinth had substituted works of the flesh for the saving truth of Jesus' sacrificial crucifixion, death, burial, and resurrection.

Baptism in water nullifies the saving power of the cross in Paul's gospel.

Paul summed up the issue in the following verse.

> *For the preaching of the cross is to those that perish foolishness, but unto us, which are saved, it is the power of God. I Corinthians 1:18*

The primary work of the ecclesia is to proclaim the cross. It is the *power of God*.

Remember that Paul stated in his letter in Romans that he was not ashamed of the gospel. The reason that he gave is as follows: In the first chapter of his letter to the Romans, Paul emphatically declared his zealous passion for his message.

> *For I am not ashamed of the gospel of Christ, for it is the power of God unto salvation to every one that believeth, to the Jew first, and also to the Greek.*

> *17For therein is the righteousness of God revealed from faith to faith: as it is written, The just shall live by faith. Romans 1:16-17*

We have reviewed and discussed some of the words of unity Paul presented in his letters. The ultimate unity at the manifestation of God's sons will shine forth in all its radiant glory, setting free the present creation from its enslavement to corruption, decay, and ruin. When sin and death entered the creation, a state of travail proceeded, producing groaning in pain akin to the birth pangs felt by women who are in the final stage of gestation, awaiting the glorious day of its release.

While we, who remain on earth as members of His body, wait in like manner in the interim for the Lord's second coming. In His first coming, He came in humility to serve as the Son of Man. In His second coming, He will appear in great majesty and power.

The body of Christ is to begin to share in advance His power in anticipation of the glory of its future service.

Jesus will begin the final phase of His saving work, which is to bring into subjection all things to the glory of the Father. His body, which currently remains on earth, will be joined by Him as His complement and helper in this majestic endeavor.

In that era, all rule, authority, and power will be put down and rendered inactive and inoperative (I Corinthians 15:24). As this era draws to a close, the members of the body of Christ are to be trained in spiritual warfare, as the enemies within are subdued by the gospel that was uniquely granted to Paul, the herald of reigning grace as the apostle to the nations.

His body, in anticipation of the saving work of the next eon, must now realize that all authority, power, and rule that are contrary to the dominion of God's kingdom must first be rendered inactive and inoperative. Each member of the body of Christ must be liberated from the hindering operation of the flesh, as it is disposed to things of the earth.

Freedom comes when believers are joined together by the truths proclaimed by Paul in his gospel. Through this binding process, the body becomes unified, standing together to prepare for Christ's return.

To enter the realm of the unities that Christ gained through His service, the body must embrace faith in God's operations through His spirit. In this manner, the mind is renewed to see with spiritual eyes. The two unities that Paul expressed are the *unity of the spirit* and *the unity of the faith*.

> *I therefore, the prisoner of the Lord, beseech you that ye walk worthy of the vocation wherewith ye are called,*
>
> *With all lowliness and meekness, with long suffering, forbearing one another in love,*
>
> *Endeavoring to keep the unity of the Spirit in the bond of peace. Ephesians 4:1-3*

We must eliminate divisions within the body. This can only occur when the spirit is brought low and meek, able to deal with other members holding up the example of Jesus and bearing with the weaknesses of others.

> *There is one body and one Spirit, even as ye are called in one hope of your calling.*
>
> *One Lord, one faith, one baptism,*
>
> *One God and Father of all, who is above all, through all, and in you all. Ephesians 4:4-6*

The word, *one,* permeates every verse. Seven times, the word is used, signifying completeness.

Any doctrine or teaching that deviate from Paul's gospel is divisive to the members of the body of Christ. It must be revealed and eliminated.

> *Now that he ascended, what is it but that he also descended first into the lower parts of the earth?*
>
> *(He that descended is the same also that ascended up far above all heavens, that he might fill all things.)*
>
> *And he gave some, apostles; and some, prophets; and some, evangelists; and some, pastors and teachers;*
>
> *For the perfecting of the saints, for the work of the ministry, for the edifying of the body of Christ:*
>
> *Till we all come in the unity of the faith, and of the knowledge of the Son of God, unto a perfect man, unto the measure of the stature of the fulness of Christ: Ephesians 4:9-13*

Five groups of gifted members contribute to the body. These members have an important and necessary responsibility.

They are to equip the body members, fully furnishing the body with truths and gifts. The members of the body are those who are to accomplish *the work of the ministry (diakonia, Strong's #G1248, attendance as a servant)*. They execute the instructions and commands of those placed above them in the Lord.

Building up the body of Christ in unity and harmony is the goal of these gifted overseers.

The ultimate goal is the *unity of faith, and the knowledge of the Son of God*. All members must believe, teach, and preach the same things that Paul proclaimed.

When teachers of God's word in this era deviate from the fulness of the gospel of Paul, divisions are sure to fracture the body, and sin has an open door to enter and despoil the unity that Christ has attained. Who can dispute this warning? Look upon the outward church and view the despicable division that abounds.

The sure and faithful results of heeding Paul's gospel in this day of declension will bring forth a *perfect man, unto the measure of the stature of the fulness of Christ.*

The question that may be asked is: Will this occur before He returns or after?

If we say "after," then just sit back and relax. You know He is coming. After all, He said through Paul not to be anxious for anything.

If we say "before," then we have plenty of spiritual ministry to complete in the body of Christ. I say, "It was before." What do you say?

At present, His body is joined to Him by the words of Paul's gospel, which speak of unity, representing the power of joining together by the truths he proclaimed. These words unite His members to Him through faith in God's declaration.

Unity within the body of Christ must be realized through significant adjustments that will mend the divisions. Repeating I Corinthians 1:10 is in order.

> *Now I beseech you, brethren, by the name of our Lord Jesus Christ, that ye all speak the same thing and that there be no divisions among you, but that ye be perfectly joined together in the same mind and in the same judgment.*

To be *perfectly joined together in the same mind and in the same judgment* is to share in the joint words of Paul's letters and not deviate by mixing and matching unconnected words and phrases. The word Paul uses in this context is *katartizo (Strong's #G2675),* meaning to complete thoroughly, i.e., to repair or adjust. This, then, is a major challenge to the church.

CHAPTER 6

THE REDEMPTION OF OUR BODIES

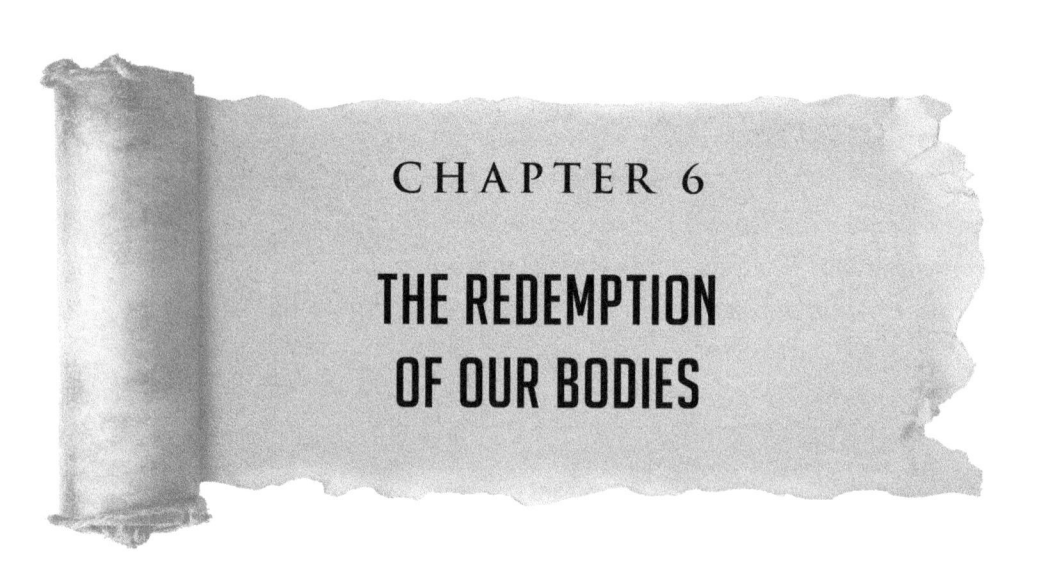

SAVED BY HOPE

> *And not only they, but ourselves also, which have the firstfruits of the Spirit, even we ourselves groan within ourselves, waiting for the adoption, to wit, the redemption of our body.*
>
> *For we are saved by hope, but hope that is seen is not hope; for what a man seeth, why doth he yet hope for? Romans 8:23,24*

Believers within the body of Christ are to be in a constant state of expectation of the Lord's return. As we have previously discussed, the manifestation of the sons of God is the crowning glory of our service to God. Also referred to as son placing, it is the focus of this waiting period as an event that we have also discussed in earlier portions of this manuscript. If you may recall, the proper word describing this event is *huiosthesia*, or son-placing.

Jesus paid the full ransom price for humanity (apolutrosis) in His death. Adam, in his defection in the garden, relinquished and forfeited his mandate to rule over the first creation on earth. Jesus, as the *last Adam*, reversed this colossal loss by redeeming humanity, as the Father included the Old Humanity in His body on the cross.

The Holy Spirit now resides in the hearts of believers in this age as proof that the New Humanity has replaced the Old. The New Humanity is being created in Christ.

The church will receive new bodies upon His return. The *redemption of our body* is guaranteed by the Spirit's presence as the earnest deposit of the Father, ensuring that every believer will put on the new body, which will be immortal and incorruptible (I Corinthians 15:53).

As for Israel, their inheritance in the next age has been secured by the death of Christ, as written in the letter to the Hebrews.

> *And for this cause, he is the mediator of the New Testament, that by means of death, for the redemption of the transgressions that were under the first testament, they, which are called, might receive the promise of eternal inheritance. Hebrews 9:15*

The death of Christ secured the redemption of the bodies of the believers, with the church being the first to receive a new body at His coming. Additionally, the death of Christ secured for the faithful believers of the nation of Israel a better resurrection. Because they did not accept a release from the extreme trials and hardships arising because of their faith concerning Christ during His visitation, a new covenant will be the testament of their inheritance upon His return for them.

> *Women received their dead raised to life again, and others were tortured, not accepting deliverance, so that they might obtain a better resurrection. Hebrews 11:35*

Israel, as God's Son to the nations, will be transformed in a special manner, equipped to minister the gospel of salvation on earth. Their hearts and minds will be changed accordingly. God's promise to them is that He will replace their stony hearts with hearts of flesh. He will write His law in their hearts and minds so that all will know Him in their reborn nation.

New bodies will be necessary for the ministry in the heavenly realms by Christ's body. This will be the total change reported by Paul in the fifth chapter of his letter in Romans.

> *And not only so, but we also find joy in God through our Lord Jesus Christ, by whom we have now received the atonement. Romans 5:11*

Atonement is the total change that God has accomplished in the death and resurrection of Christ. At present, His relationship has changed from estrangement to absolute unity with humanity. We now know by faith of His wondrous operation when He raised Jesus from the dead.

The change *(katallage)* will be visibly realized upon His return, when the old, dying, weak, and sinful body acquired from Adam will be permanently put off and the new vigorous, dynamic, incorruptible, and immortal body will be put on.

In the final portion of chapter 8 of Paul's letter to the Romans, these wondrous events are pronounced as the hope of believers in this age.

Paul's letter to the Romans contains the foundation of faith for all believers in this time of reigning grace. Chapter 8 of the letter unfolds the stunning future of the sons of God as they join Christ Jesus as the head of the body. In the previous chapters, we discussed the unity that will exist between the Father and His only begotten son, Jesus, our Lord.

Also, we discussed the absolute unity that will be expressed by the members of His body with Him as well as with each other. The sons of God will be manifested to join in His radiant glory.

Romans, Chapter 8, discloses and clarifies the work of God's Holy Spirit in bringing many sons into glory. Intercession on behalf of the body of Christ by the Spirit will be an indispensable service to the body, as the deep things of God will be one of the major subjects of the Spirit's prayers to God.

Walking in the *newness of life* is made possible by the knowing, reckoning, and yielding described in Romans 6:1–13. In Romans, chapter 7, Paul claimed that believers should *serve in newness of spirit (Romans 7:6)* in so far as, in the death of Christ's body, believers are exempt from the law.

Righteousness is reckoned based on faith and not on works of the law.

Holy spiritual fruit can now be expressed since the members are not to serve in the *oldness of the letter* but in the *newness of spirit (Romans 7:6)*.

In Romans 6, the *body of sin* is rendered idle (Romans 6:6) as the *old man is crucified with him.* In Romans 7, believers are delivered from this *wretched man, the body of this death,* thanking our Lord, Jesus Christ, so that with the mind we can *serve the law of God.* The flesh, however, continues to serve *the law of sin* (Romans 7:24 –25) when we attempt to produce fruit by means of the flesh.

As our study and discussion move into Romans 8, Paul assists the believer who has completed the journey through Romans 6 and 7 by redefining the walk of faith as a new expression of service.

> *There is therefore now no condemnation to them, who are in Christ Jesus, who walk not after the flesh but after the Spirit. Romans 8:1*

The enlightened believer is enabled to walk in this newness by the operation of a new law within the believer's heart. This new operative law is transmitted to the spirit man within as *the law of the Spirit of Life in Christ Jesus*. The new man is liberated by being exempt from moral liability for the ceremonial observance of the outward requirements of the written law. Such vain observance in prior attempts at service was contaminated by *the law of sin and death (Romans 8:2).*

The believer's walk in the world has taken on new focus and dimension. A spiritual accomplishment has occurred inside the enlightened heart, where the inner new man resides. A new element of service is at hand. The old has given way to the new.

> *For what the law could not do, in that it was weak through the flesh, God sent his own Son in the likeness of sinful flesh, and for sin, condemned sin in the flesh: Romans 8:3*

God's own Son, in the likeness of sinful flesh and for sin, condemned sin in the flesh. I have repeated the last portion of the above verse for emphasis. The fulfillment of the outward law—holy, just, and good—could not be walked out by the formal observance of the law. Sin in the flesh was the hindrance, keeping those who attempted to obey the law in the flesh in bondage to sin. Now, Christ's victory has condemned sin in the flesh. The righteous requirements of the law are still in effect. But now the fulfillment can be accomplished inwardly by those who are walking after the Spirit and not after the flesh (Romans 8:4).

Every person is comprised of three parts, which are the spirit, soul, and body. The spirit comes from God, the Father of spirits. The physical body comes from the soil of the earth. When the two major components, the body and spirit, are united, they form the expression of the soul.

The redemption of the body occurs at the time of rejoining the spirit with a new body. This redemption will be experienced by the members of Christ's body who remain alive on earth until He comes and by those of Him who have tasted death in His absence. The dead in Christ will be raised first and then immediately joined with members who are alive, caught up together in the air where the Lord appears.

> *For this we say unto you by the word of the Lord, that we which are alive and remain unto the coming of the Lord shall not prevent them which are asleep.*
>
> *For the Lord himself shall descend from heaven with a shout, with the voice of the archangel, and with the trump of God; and the dead in Christ shall rise first:*
>
> *Then we which are alive and remain shall be caught up together with them in the clouds, to meet the Lord in the air, and so shall we ever be with the Lord.*
>
> *Therefore, comfort one another with these words. I Thessalonians 4:15–18*

While awaiting His return and the redemption of our bodies, spiritual blessings in the heavenly places are described by the joint words that connect us to Christ during this time of expectation. As we move into Paul's letter to the Ephesians, he reveals these blessings through various *sun* words that describe how the body participates in His ministry from the heavens.

> *Even when we were dead in sins, hath quickened us together with Christ (by grace ye are saved).*
>
> *And hath raised us up together and made us sit together in heavenly places in Christ Jesus.*

> *In the ages to come, he might shew the exceeding riches of his grace in his kindness toward us through Christ Jesus.*
>
> *For by grace are ye saved through faith, and that is not of yourselves; it is the gift of God. Not of works, lest any man should boast.*
>
> *For we are his workmanship, created in Christ Jesus unto good works, which God hath before ordained that we should walk in them. Ephesians 2:5-10*

The initial verse above is worthy of comment. Offenses are a form of sin being related to relationships that have been severed. When humanity was put to death in Christ, we became dead to both sin and offense.

Being dead, God brought the New Humanity to life when He brought Christ back to life *(suzoopoieo, Strong's #4806, to reanimate conjointly with)*. This is a result of His overwhelming grace in the saving work of Christ.

Ephesians 2:5 presents two spiritual facts. The body of Christ, as the New Humanity in Him, has been raised up in Him *(sunergeiro, Strong's #4891, to rouse from death in company with) a*nd seated in the heavenlies together in Him *(sugkathizo, Strong's #4776, to give a seat in company with)*.

These spiritual truths link believers to Christ in heaven. Where He is, we are there in Him, in spirit.

Paul clarifies these truths in his letter to the Colossian Assembly. He instructs believers to be mentally disposed in a heavenly direction.

> *If ye then be risen with Christ, seek those things which are above, where Christ sitteth on the right hand of God.*
>
> *Set your affection on things above, not on things on the earth.*

> *For ye are dead, and your life is hid with Christ in God.*
>
> *When Christ, who is our life, shall appear, then shall ye also appear with him in glory. Colossians 3:1-4*

You have died off in the *last Adam,* in the Old Humanity. Christ became the complete representative of Old Humanity in flesh on His cross. He became sin so that we might become the righteousness of God in Him (II Corinthians 5:21). He died for us, as sinners, displaying the magnitude of God's love (5:8).

Because He represented all humanity, every human in the past, in the present, and being born in the future is included in the operation of God in Christ.

As He was roused and stood up in life again, all of humanity, now considered the New Humanity, became alive in Him as the head of the New Humanity. Your state of possessing vitality is *hid with Christ in God.*

Before Christ revealed His saving work of the New Creation to Paul, there existed a pronounced division between the Jewish believers, those of the circumcision, and the Gentile believers, those of the uncircumcision. Paul's ministry to the churches, both through his letters and in person, was in large part directed towards tearing down the barriers between them.

Paul sought unity on behalf of the Father and His Son, Jesus, the Savior of all.

His explanation of the spiritual unification of these two disparate spiritual groups of humanity is worthy of serious consideration. The glory of the spiritual enlightenment is magnified when considering Paul's vehement hatred towards the members of the sect of the *way (Acts 9:2),* which he felt as Saul of Tarsus, on behalf of his loyalty to his nation and his heritage.

Saul of Tarsus, later named Paul after his conversion, was the consummate Jewish hater of Christians.

Adding to the animosity of the inbred hostility of the Jewish heart towards the heathen of the nations, Saul was the perfect zealot fiercely dedicated to the goal of eliminating Jesus' faithful followers. By a total Holy Spirit renovation within him, Saul of Tarsus had a remarkable transformation when Christ Jesus met him on the way to Damascus.

Paul saw things with new spiritual eyes as he wrote to the church at Ephesus, which was comprised mainly of Gentiles of the nations.

> *Wherefore remember, that ye being in time past Gentiles in the flesh, who are called uncircumcision by that which is called circumcision in the flesh made by hands;*
>
> *At that time, ye were without Christ, aliens from the commonwealth of Israel, strangers from the covenants of promise, having no hope, and without God in the world.*
>
> *But now, in Christ Jesus, ye who were sometimes far off, are made near by the blood of Christ. For he is our peace, who hath made both one and hath broken down the middle wall of partition between us;*
>
> *Having abolished in his flesh the enmity, even the law of commandments contained in ordinances; for to make in himself of twain one new man, so making peace;*
>
> *And that he might reconcile both unto God in one body by the cross, having slain the enmity thereby:*
>
> *And came and preached peace to you which were afar off, and to them that were nigh.*

> *For through him we both have access by one Spirit unto the Father.*
> Ephesians 2:11-18

Jesus, on His cross, reconciled humanity to God. The enmity that God placed within the humans of the garden was eliminated by the death of His Son. Additionally, the enmity between Jews and Gentiles was also eliminated in Christ's body *by the cross, having slain the enmity thereby.*

As every accomplishment of the Lord is to be realized by faith as we await His appearing, these spiritual blessings enumerated by Paul must be believed as well. Being justified, we are to spiritually proceed from faith to faith.

The division that exists in the world is common to all of humanity. The people of the earth may be divided by race. They may be divided by sex. They may be divided by age. The members of humanity may be divided by religious preference. It makes no difference. Division by matters of the flesh is in opposition to God's purpose.

Unity in Christ creates a proper division that is acceptable to God. People are either *in Adam* or *in Christ*. All begin in the first group, in Adam. All are to end in the second, in Christ. The Lord came to earth to bring a division between the flesh and the spirit.

> *Think not that I came to send peace on earth; I came not to send peace, but a sword.* Matthew 10:34

There is proper division and separation. There is also a proper unity. Gentile believers are no longer separated from the commonwealth of Israel. In Christ, as the Old Humanity was taken to the cross, crucified with Christ, then buried with Him in the tomb. In the darkness of the grave, the New Humanity came forth in Christ. All believers in this current age are to identify with His death, followed by identification with His life.

The Old Humanity has been placed into death, Christ's death. There is now a new creation in Christ. The New Humanity was created in Him as He was raised from the dead. Faith in the declarations of God links believers to these truths.

God, the Father, has provided this holy division. The Old have passed. All things have become new in Him who was raised from the dead.

Now mutual access is provided to the Father through Christ in one Spirit.

> *And they are built upon the foundation of the apostles and prophets, Jesus Christ himself being the chief corner stone;*
>
> *(I see that the building (singular, not plural) is what is meant here) In whom all the buildings fitly framed together groweth unto a holy temple in the Lord:*
>
> *In whom ye also are built together for a habitation of God through the Spirit. Ephesians 2:20-22*

Unity has been attained, in one Spirit, by Christ's cross. The holy building is a temple that rests on the foundation laid by the apostles and prophets. Jesus Christ is the chief cornerstone. All those living in Him are living stones.

The living stones are being connected *(sunarmologeo, Strong's #4883, to render close jointed together, organize compactly)*. The temple is being erected by Christ. The members are being built together *(sunoikodomeo, Strong's #4925, to construct in company with other believers)* into a dwelling place of God in spirit.

Therefore, the Gentile believers are fellow citizens with the saints, as it is written by Paul;

> *Now therefore ye are no more strangers and foreigners, but fellow citizens with the saints and of the household of God; Ephesians 2:19*

The word for fellow citizens is *sumpolites (Strong's #G4847)*. It pertains to citizens who jointly possess the same citizenship as others. In this case, they are the people who are consecrated by the Spirit to God. The Gentiles are also relatives of God, related in spirit to all others who are kindred of the faith.

Paul was a prisoner of Jesus Christ for the Gentiles, as believing members of the body. He is acting as an administrator of the household of God with oversight of the management of the grace given to him by God.

> *For this cause, I, Paul, the prisoner of Jesus Christ for you Gentiles,*
>
> *If ye have heard of the dispensation of the grace of God that has been given to you, How that by revelation he made known unto me the mystery; as I wrote afore in a few words,*
>
> *Whereby, when ye read, ye may understand my knowledge in the mystery of Christ.*
>
> *Which in other ages was not made known unto the sons of men, as it is now revealed unto his holy apostles and prophets by the Spirit; Ephesians 3:1-5*

Paul explained to the church at Corinth that within the body of Christ there is an office of responsibility afforded to all as administrators of the mysteries of God (I Corinthians 4:1). In these verses, he is exercising the duties of the office and discussing the *mystery of Christ*.

This revelation has been disclosed to Paul by Christ to be administered to the church of this age, being revealed *to his holy apostles and prophets by the Spirit.* In prior ages, this mystery was not revealed, as the time of its disclosure was not yet at hand.

This part of the mystery of Christ is revealed in the following verse.

> *That the Gentiles should be fellow heirs, of the same body, and partakers of his promise in Christ by the gospel. Ephesians 3:6*

These spiritual truths magnify the glory of the unity that is made in the death of God's Son, as the Son of Man. The Old Humanity has been nullified through Christ's cross. The enmity between the Jewish believers and the Gentile believers has been eliminated in the flesh of Christ, as He was nailed to the cross and then placed into death.

The gospel has united the Gentiles as fellow heirs *(sugkleronomos, Strong's #G4789.)* A co-heir, of the same body *(sussomos, Strong's #G4954, of a joint body)*, and partakers *(summetochos, Strong's #G4830, a co-participant)* of his promise in Christ by the gospel.

> *I was made a minister according to the gift of the grace of God given to me by the effective working of his power. Unto me, who am less than the least of all saints, is this grace given that I should preach among the Gentiles the unsearchable riches of Christ;*
>
> *And to make all men see what is the fellowship of the mystery, which from the beginning of the world hath been hid in God, who created all things by Jesus Christ:*
>
> *To the intent that now the principalities and powers in heavenly places might be known by the church as the manifold wisdom of God,*
>
> *According to the eternal purpose that he purposed in Christ Jesus, our Lord. Ephesians 3:7-11*

The members of the church as it now exists are called to first understand and believe that they are included in Christ's crucifixion and death, which effectively put the old humanity in a neutral state, no longer allowing sin to be its master. Accordingly, the joint truths of Paul's gospel are to be embraced by faith, which unites the members of the joint body.

They, as a collective unit, are to function in that unity, having fellowship with each other as its saving power. This fellowship of the mystery of Christ is to be revealed through the church during this current eon and beyond. It has been hidden in God as another grand truth that is to be proclaimed, revealing the wisdom of God veiled throughout the prior ages.

This has been God's purpose for the ages. He purposed this in Christ Jesus.

The *principalities and powers in heavenly places* are viewing the manifold wisdom of God through the church as the mystery of Christ is revealed to the body of Christ. He is both the Son of God and the Son of Man.

Our first glimpse of this divine plan was implemented through Moses in the priestly service within the Tabernacle in the wilderness. In the Holy Place within the tent, upon a table of the presence, twelve loaves of bread were on display. These loaves began to speak of something far more revealing than just the twelve tribes of Israel.

The word *purpose (prothesis, Strong's #G4286)* in the eleventh verse quoted above is a noun, meaning a setting forth, figuratively revealing a link to God's intention. The showbread in the temple is part of this divine expression.

God was placing in view His divine purpose, which would be fully expressed in Jesus Christ, God's only begotten Son, as the Son of Man, redeeming the old humanity from the realm of darkness and having created in Himself the new humanity. It is the duty of the church to display this truth in the unity of the spirit and the unity of the faith.

> *In whom we have boldness and access with confidence by the faith of him.*
>
> *Wherefore I desire that ye faint not at my tribulations for you, which is your glory.*
>
> *For this cause, I bow my knees to the Father of our Lord Jesus Christ.*
>
> *Of whom the whole family in heaven and earth is named,*
>
> *That he would grant you, according to the riches of his glory, to be strengthened with might by his Spirit in the inner man;*
>
> *That Christ may dwell in your hearts by faith; that ye, being rooted and grounded in love,*
>
> *May be able to comprehend with all saints what is the breadth, length, depth, and height; And to know the love of Christ, which passeth knowledge, that ye might be filled with all the fulness of God.*
>
> *Now unto him that is able to do exceedingly abundant above all that we ask or think, according to the power that worketh in us,*
>
> *Unto him be glory in the church by Christ Jesus throughout all ages, world without end. Amen. Ephesians 3:12-21*

There is the outer man, and there is the inner man. The outer man is dictated to by the flesh, which is connected to this world. The inner man is directed by the spirit, which is the true essence of our being, and is connected to the heavenly realm by the Holy Spirit that resides within every believer.

When the redemption of our bodies occurs at His second coming, our new outer body will be fully in tune with the spiritual man within. The current conflict between our old flesh and the spirit will no longer hinder our service to God.

Before anyone is called by God, the soul and the body direct the acts of a person as the inner desires arise from the stony heart. The passions and lusts within the heart are influenced by the spirit of the world, as Paul explained in his letter to the church, Ephesus.

> *And you hath he quickened, who were dead in trespasses and sins;*
>
> *Wherein in time past ye walked according to the course of this world, according to the prince of the power of the air, the spirit that now worketh in the children of disobedience:*
>
> *Among whom also we all had our conversation in times past in the lusts of our flesh, fulfilling the desires of the flesh and of the mind; and were by nature the children of wrath, even as others.*
>
> *But God, who is rich in mercy, for his great love wherewith he loved us,*
>
> *Even when we were dead in sins, hath quickened us together with Christ, (by grace ye are saved;)*
>
> *And hath raised us up together, and made us sit together in heavenly places in Christ Jesus:*
>
> *That in the ages to come he might shew the exceeding riches of his grace in his kindness toward us through Christ Jesus. Ephesians 2:1-7*

We, as believing members of His body, have been quickened together *(suzoopoieo)*, raised up together *(sunegeiro)* and are seated together *(sunkathizo)* in the heavenly places because the new humanity is in Christ, and wherever He is, the body is in Him. The celestial powers and authorities could not perceive this wondrous truth until God revealed it to Paul. Spiritual truths for the body's edification are revealed by Paul through his gospel.

In the eons to come, the cohesive joint body will be made evident and will show forth His surpassing riches of grace. Moral excellence will be demonstrated toward us in and through Christ Jesus.

> *For by grace are ye saved through faith, and that is not of yourselves; it is the gift of God. Not of works, lest any man should boast.*
>
> *For we are his workmanship, created in Christ Jesus unto good works, which God hath before ordained that we should walk in them. Ephesians 2:8-10*

The body of Christ is His present achievement *(poiema, Strong's #G4161, that which has been made)*. The same word has been used in Paul's letter to the Romans.

> *For the invisible things of him from the creation of the world are clearly seen, being understood by the things that are made, even his eternal power and Godhead, so that they are without excuse: Romans 1:20.*

That which was made in the first creation—the stars, the planets, the earth, the land, the seas, and all the plants and animals—reveals two major invisible things about God, which are His power and the order of the system portraying His divinity. And now, in the second creation, the New Humanity fashioned in Christ is being conformed to the image of God mirrored in the image of Christ. The basic spiritual matters, being things of consequence, of Paul's gospel came first. The deep spiritual things are now coming into view, which are displaying His chief characteristic, His overwhelming love.

The body of Christ plays a dual role, one which is carried out on earth as His second coming is anticipated, and the other role will be realized when the body will walk in the splendor of being a part of Him in new bodies created in Christ Jesus.

Paul, in his letter to the Colossians, stresses the importance of not being drawn back into the world, especially into religious observances practiced through the traditions of men.

> *Beware lest any man spoil you through philosophy and vain deceit, after the tradition of men, after the rudiments of the world, and not after Christ.*
>
> *For in him dwelleth all the fulness of the Godhead bodily.*
>
> *And ye are complete in him, who is the head of all principality and power. In whom also ye are circumcised with the circumcision made without hands, in putting off the body of the sins of the flesh by the circumcision of Christ:*
>
> *Buried with him in baptism, wherein also ye are risen with him through the faith of the operation of God, who hath raised him from the dead.*
>
> *And you, being dead in your sins and the uncircumcision of your flesh, hath he quickened together with him, having forgiven you all trespasses;*
>
> *Blotting out the handwriting of ordinances that were against us, which was contrary to us, and taking it out of the way, nailing it to his cross;*
>
> *And having spoiled principalities and powers, he made a shew of them openly, triumphing over them in it.*

> *Let no man therefore judge you in meat, or in drink, or in respect of a holy day, or of the new moon, or of the Sabbath days.*
>
> *Which are shadow of things to come, but the body is of Christ. Colossians 2:8-17*

Paul cannot urge us any stronger to remain observant of the spiritual guidance of the inner man who is being changed by means of Paul's gospel. The outer man is not to be configured to the current eon by following the empty religion of the old humanity, but to be transfigured by renewal of the mind, whereby true godly worship is made possible (Romans 12:1-2).

In the previous verses in the second chapter of Paul's letter to the Colossians, Paul uses *sun* words that emphasize the joint nature of Christ's victory as applied to the entire body of Christ as one cohesive unit. In Him, the entire complement of the deity dwells in bodily form. In Him, the body is being filled to the fullest, as He is the head of the body over every sovereignty and authority.

In Him, a circumcision has occurred, not by the work of hands as to the cutting of the physical flesh, but by the operation of God through the stripping off the body of the sins of the flesh in the circumcision of Christ.

By faith, the members of His body realize that all have been placed in the tomb with Him *(sunthapto)* which led also to being awakened with Him *(susoopoieo)* by the operation of God, the One awakening Him out of the ones in the abode of the dead. Being counted among the dead by the offenses and the uncircumcision of the flesh, He makes all to live together with Him, having dealt graciously with all the offenses.

He also erased the handwriting that was against us, containing the decrees hostile to us, and has taken it away, nailing it to the cross. Therefore, He spoiled the sovereignties and authorities by making a public show of them, boldly triumphing over them.

> *If ye then be risen with Christ, seek those things which are above, where Christ sitteth on the right hand of God.*
>
> *Set your affection on things above, not on things on earth. Or ye are dead, and your life is hid with Christ in God. Colossians 3:1-3*

We were roused together *(sunegeiro)*, in company with Christ. Our affections, concerns, and interests are for heavenly things, not for the things of this earth.

We died. Our lives have been hidden with Christ in God.

These spiritual facts describe our current reality in the heavenly realms, which is to transform our minds, creating a disposition that is set on the spirit and not on the flesh (Romans 8:5, 6).

The proper spiritual mindset leads to life and peace. We, therefore, believe in and have a genuine expectation of what lies ahead.

> *When Christ, who is our life, shall appear, then shall ye also appear with him in glory. Colossians 3:4*

Armed with the overpowering prospect of sharing His victory when He returns, we are to walk out these truths and follow Paul's express instructions.

> *Mortify therefore your members which are upon the earth; fornication, uncleanness, inordinate affection, evil concupiscence, and covetousness, which is idolatry: Colossians 3:5*

Paul instructs believers to deprive the parts of the physical body of the power that comes from sin and death.

> [8] *But now ye also put off all these; anger, wrath, malice, blasphemy, filthy communication out of your mouth.*
>
> [9] *Lie not one to another, seeing that ye have **put off the old man** with his deeds;*
>
> [10] *And have **put on the new man**, which is renewed in knowledge after the image of him that created him:*
>
> [11] *Where there is neither Greek nor Jew, circumcision nor uncircumcision, Barbarian, Scythian, bond nor free: but Christ is all, and in all.*
>
> *Put on therefore, as the elect of God, holy and beloved, bowels of mercies, kindness, humbleness of mind, meekness, long suffering;*
>
> [13] *Forbearing one another, and forgiving one another, if any man have a quarrel against any: even as Christ forgave you, so also do ye.*
>
> [14] *And above all these things put on charity, which is the bond of perfectness.*
>
> [15] *And let the peace of God rule in your hearts, to the which also ye are called in one body; and be ye thankful.*
>
> [16] *Let the word of Christ dwell in you richly in all wisdom; teaching and admonishing one another in psalms and hymns and spiritual songs, singing with grace in your hearts to the Lord.*
>
> [17] *And whatsoever ye do in word or deed, do all in the name of the Lord Jesus, giving thanks to God and the Father by him.*

He summarizes his instructions to the church in an all-inclusive statement.

> ²³*And whatsoever ye do, do it heartily, as to the Lord, and not unto men;*
>
> ²⁴*Knowing that of the Lord ye shall receive the reward of the inheritance: for ye serve the Lord Christ.*

God placed Adam in the garden to serve and protect his allotment with the help of his mate, Eve. Likewise, the New Humanity is to enter divine service, awaiting the return of the Lord. The church is the body of Christ. Israel is the companion of the church to minister to the nations to fulfill their calling.

CHAPTER 7

SONS OF ADAM/ADAM'S DEATH
SONS OF GOD/THE DEATH OF CHRIST

Grace reigns for believers in this age because of Christ's death and resurrection. It is evident that some of those who heard Paul's gospel didn't understand portions of it, concluding that they could continue to allow sin to reign so that *grace may abound*. This erroneous mindset revealed a feeble lack of knowledge concerning the elements of his gospel message.

> *[19] For as by one man's disobedience many were made sinners, so by the obedience of one shall many be made righteous.*
>
> *[20] Moreover the law entered, that the offence might abound. But where sin abounded, grace did much more abound: Romans 5:19-20*

Paul emphatically stated in the first verses of Romans 6 that the fallacy of such reasoning was due to a definite misunderstanding of the truth concerning the death of Christ. Let's look again at that section of Paul's letter.

> *[1] What shall we say then? Shall we continue in sin, that grace may abound?*
>
> *[2] God forbid. How shall we, that are dead to sin, live any longer therein?*

> ³*Know ye not, that so many of us as were baptized into Jesus Christ were baptized into his death? Romans 6:1-3*

These verses contain positive facts about Christ that applied to believers who received Paul's gospel. Specifically, Paul claimed that they are *dead to sin,* and that their death to sin is explicitly true since, as believers, they have been *baptized into Jesus Christ.* Being baptized into Him they *were baptized into his death.*

These dynamic gospel truths provide a vital power in the hearts of those who embrace Paul's life-changing message. Victory over sin can only be accomplished by the death of Christ.

God, the Father, terminated the reign of sin over humanity through the sacrificial death of His Son. Paul, spiritually enlightened to these wondrous truths, sets them forth in his marvelous chapter in his Romans letter to liberate believers from the bondage of sin.

He continues to herald the victory over sin by using the exact terms of Christ's triumph:

> ⁴*Therefore we are <u>buried with him</u> by baptism into death: that like as Christ was raised up from the dead by the glory of the Father, even so we also should walk in newness of life.*
>
> ⁵*For if we have been <u>planted together</u> in the likeness of his death, we shall be also in the likeness of his resurrection:*
>
> ⁶*Knowing this, that our old man is <u>crucified with him</u>, that the body of sin might be destroyed, that henceforth we should not serve sin.*
>
> ⁷*For he that is dead is freed from sin.*

> *⁸Now if we be dead with Christ, we believe that we shall also <u>live with</u> him:*
>
> *⁹Knowing that Christ being raised from the dead dieth no more; death hath no more dominion over him.*
>
> *¹⁰For in that he died, he died unto sin once: but in that he liveth, he liveth unto God. Romans 6:4-10*

Therein, matchless truths are expressed through exact Greek words of unity. Paul expresses each spiritual truth by employing precise words that perfectly define correct thoughts of the mind of God concerning Christ's sacrificial death. These are words of unity illustrating accurately that which the Father accomplished through the death of His beloved Son.

The particular words are listed in the Appendix of this manuscript as they appear in Paul's letters. For reference, the *sun* words in the above section of Romans, chapter 6, are underlined representing the Greek words, *sunthapto, sumphusos, sustauroo, and suzao.*

God, the Father, through Christ's death, has attained a total change in His relationship with humanity. He has introduced a completely new humanity in Christ, ending the *old humanity* through the death and burial of His beloved Son, and creating the *new humanity* in the new life and resurrection of Jesus Christ, who is the first-born from death.

God, the Father, has taken the conciliatory step necessary to affect the change in the relationship between Himself and Adam's family. The entire human race as enemies of God due to the enmity within each heart has been fully conciliated by the death of God's Son.

The *old humanity* was crucified with Christ and buried with Him. The *new humanity as* created in Christ is now alive in Him.

His death is an ongoing reality. Believers are to receive the *total change* described in Romans 5:11.

> *[11]Not only is this so, but we also boast in God through our Lord Jesus Christ, through whom we have now received reconciliation. Romans 5:11 NIV*

The King James Version did not assist the believer in understanding the *reconciliation* referring to the act as the *atonement*, which speaks of the covering over of sins by the blood of Christ. Additionally, the NIV as cited above falls short of the true meaning of what God, the Father, has accomplished in the *death of His Son*.

A more correct and meaningful English word when translating the Greek word, *katallage*, is *conciliation*. This rich and vibrant word describes a total change between two estranged people in a relationship that has been broken. However, it is a one-sided change pertaining to the one side that has taken the *conciliatory* step in mending the broken relationship. Hopefully, the *conciliatory* act of the one will impact on the other estranged party causing a complete and total re*conciliation*.

In this case, as Paul proclaims in his Romans letter that God, the Father, has taken the step of *conciliation* when He dispatched His beloved Son to die on behalf of humanity.

> *[10]For if, while we were God's enemies, we were reconciled to him through the death of his Son, how much more, having been reconciled, shall we be saved through his life! Romans 5:10*

In the mending of a broken relationship, the *conciliation* comes first. And when received in a grateful heart by the one being *conciliated*, the *reconciliation* follows, bringing the two parties together again.

The estrangement between humanity and God began in the garden where Adam sided with the Adversary and ate the fruit from the tree that God had reserved for a later time and purpose. The fruit that was withheld from the couple represented the knowledge of good and evil, which would be both vital and valuable towards their growth towards maturity. But the Lord God undoubtedly did not mean for them to gain the benefits until they were able to use it to better serve Him.

The Adversary offered a quick fix, a shortcut to wisdom by eating the fruit. The deception aroused within Eve the desire to gain the wisdom that God's enemy falsely claimed was being unduly denied. The opponent of God made Him appear to arbitrarily withhold His grace.

Wisdom was going to come from God, in His time, and through His nurture and oversight. But they couldn't wait, and so they ate.

When Adam disobeyed, fellowship with God was immediately broken, but humanity's ultimate redemption was a vital part of God's salvation plan. Adam's race would ultimately be redeemed through the Father's wisdom and grace and Jesus Christ's sacrificial obedience.

The Father and His beloved Son will regain their fallen family.

The critical step towards reunification was taken when the Father sent His Son to die for His enemies. God knew that Adam's race of hostile combatants was both unwilling and unable to adjust their broken relationship with Him. He took the initiative of the total change by ending the *old humanity* in the death of His Son and beginning the *new humanity* in Christ's resurrection into new life.

Paul, the apostle to the nations, was thoroughly schooled in all the varied facets of Christ's victory. He received his gospel directly from Christ Jesus, not from any human source. As he assimilated the inestimable truths of his gospel message, he realized that the grandeur of God's infinite grace far exceeds the limited glory of the law of God through the Mosaic tablets which he once strongly defended.

Paul realized that no sin descends man so deep in despair that God's love cannot reach down and rescue him by His grace. Adam's disobedience and its universal effect on humanity would be more than countered by His infinite grace and the gift of His grace through the unwavering obedience of Christ Jesus our Lord.

Paul's life-changing gospel may fall on deaf ears and hardened hearts by far too many who hear amiss his proclamation of victory. The failure to grasp the essence of his announcements may affect many, but God's vast love will overcome all resistance in the end.

We see in the final verses of Romans 5 that many simply did not understand what he said about grace exceeding sin.

> *¹⁹For as by one man's disobedience many were made sinners, so by the obedience of one shall many be made righteous.*
>
> *²⁰Moreover the law entered, that the offence might abound. But where sin abounded, grace did much more abound:*
>
> *²¹That as sin hath reigned unto death, even so might grace reign through righteousness unto eternal life by Jesus Christ our Lord. Romans 5:19-21*

If you heard and believed what Paul just said, you would marvel at the superlative nature of grace. Sin once reigned unto death but now grace is reigning through righteousness by Jesus Christ, Paul's Lord, and our Lord. To those who didn't fully grasp Paul's meaning, they may have erroneously reasoned that they should continue in sin that grace may abound! Paul responds to that mistaken conclusion as follows in Romans, chapter six.

> *What shall we say then? Shall we continue in sin, that grace may abound?*
>
> *²God forbid. How shall we, that are dead to sin, live any longer therein?*
>
> *³Know ye not, that so many of us as were baptized into Jesus Christ were baptized into his death? Romans 6:1-3*

Here is the halleluiah chorus!

We, as believers, are to realize that we *were baptized into his death.*

This is our victory cry concerning sin.

We are *baptized into Jesus Christ!*

God's proclamation through Paul clearly states that we were baptized into his death!

This is a pronouncement of the Lord's total victory over sin. It is His death into which we were baptized. How many? All of humanity according to Romans 6, verse 6.

The spiritual effect of Christ's death over sin is through the faith of Christ that Paul was given, which is also equally effective to all who are given the same faith and believe the message that Paul proclaims.

We must, then, gain greater knowledge about His death. We are to identify other wondrous facts that Paul realized when Jesus graciously blessed him. For the remainder of his service to the Lord, Paul's mission was to fully educate his fellow laborers concerning the death and the conquering life of our Lord.

Christ's Death has changed everything.

Christ's victorious truth, expressed through love by the members of His body, with Him as the Head, will subdue all rule, power and authority.

We testify as to the total change God, our Father, has gracefully accomplished through Christ

Our sins have been covered over by Christ's *blood*.

We are enabled to *walk in newness of life*.

We are no longer enemies of God, but are conciliated to Him by the *death of His Son*.

The *old humanity has been crucified with Christ*.

The *body of sin* has been rendered idle.

We are dead to the law by the *body of Christ*.

We are enabled to *serve in newness of Spirit, and not in oldness of the letter*.

We thank God through Jesus Christ our Lord, *who shall deliver me from the body of this death*.

There is therefore now no condemnation to them which are in Christ Jesus.

The law of the Spirit of life in Christ Jesus math made me free from the law of sin and death.

The righteousness of the law might be fulfilled in us who walk not after the flesh, but after the spirit.

We are becoming *spiritually minded* which is *life and peaee*.

The Spirit of him that raised up Jesus from the dead dwells in us.

Therefore, the Spirit *shall also quicken our mortal bodies by his Spirit that dwells in us.*

We are enabled *through the Spirit to mortify the deeds of the body,* by which we shall live.

In all these things we are more than conquerors through him that loved us.

Nothing *shall be able to separate us from the love of God, which is in Christ Jesus our Lord.*

Genuine, fruit-bearing spiritual service from believers, who view their spiritual standing as joined to the Savior, embrace the liberating truths of Paul's gospel.

Believers who see themselves as being in Christ Jesus, see that His death is their death, and His life is their life.

Paul's entreaty to the sons of God who are being led by the Spirit speaks loudly and clearly in Romans, chapter 12.

> *[1] I beseech you therefore, brethren, by the mercies of God, that ye present your bodies a living sacrifice, holy, acceptable unto God, which is your reasonable service.*
>
> *[2] And be not conformed to this world: but be ye transformed by the renewing of your mind, that ye may prove what is that good, and acceptable, and perfect, will of God.*
>
> *[3] For I say, through the grace given unto me, to every man that is among you, not to think of himself more highly than he ought to think; but to think soberly, according as God hath dealt to every man the measure of faith. Romans 12:1-3*

The presentation of our bodies to God can now be viewed as a *living sacrifice,* which describes our *reasonable service.*

Such proper service shuns conformity to the world as the mind is being renewed. Believers in Christ discern God's will for their daily sacrifice, testing his good will, his acceptable will, and his perfect will.

Paul's gospel message, taken in its full expression, continues to adjust their faith towards maturity. The renewed mind coupled with genuine humility encourages believers to offer themselves to God, as alive from the dead.

The measure of faith that all believers receive begins as small as a mustard seed. Successive levels of faith are attained as Paul's gospel is preached in its fullness.

The truths, containing the power of God unto salvation, are presented in Paul's letters in the New Testament in a certain order. As we rely on that order to obtain a sequential presentation of his timeless gospel, the next in order is his I Corinthians letter.

Paul reminds the Corinthian believers that they have been *called into the fellowship of his Son Jesus Christ our Lord.* Based on that calling, Paul instructs the Corinthian believers that they *be perfectly joined together in the same mind and in the same judgement. I Corinthians 1:9-10*

The same instructions are meant for every believer throughout the administration of righteousness, which continues in this era of reigning grace. Paul's gospel must be taught in its entirety. Nothing should be left out, and nothing should be added.

Division must be vigorously opposed. Every facet of his gospel must be proclaimed. Otherwise, the faith that was once delivered unto the saints will fade and be replaced by the traditions of men.

Paul soon realized that he was not sent to administer water baptism. The saving message must focus on the cross of Christ.

> *¹⁷For Christ sent me not to baptize, but to preach the gospel: not with wisdom of words, lest the cross of Christ should be made of none effect.*
>
> *¹⁸For the preaching of the cross is to them that perish foolishness; but unto us which are saved it is the power of God. I Corinthians 1:17-18*

Further, they were instructed as to the concentration on the cross as proclaimed by Paul.

> *²²For the Jews require a sign, and the Greeks seek after wisdom:*
>
> *²³But we preach Christ crucified, unto the Jews a stumblingblock, and unto the Greeks foolishness;*
>
> *²⁴But unto them which are called, both Jews and Greeks, Christ the power of God, and the wisdom of God.*
>
> *²⁵Because the foolishness of God is wiser than men; and the weakness of God is stronger than men. I Corinthians 1:20-25*

Christ crucified is the crucial point of Paul's gospel, which magnifies *Christ the power of God, and the wisdom of God.*

> *³⁰But of him are ye in Christ Jesus, who of God is made unto us wisdom, and righteousness, and sanctification, and redemption:*
>
> *³¹That, according as it is written, He that glorieth, let him glory in the Lord. I Corinthianss 1:30-31*

There could not have been a more precise introduction to Paul's clear message to the Corinthians. Departure from this message would result in a diminished emphasis on what Christ means to His saints; *wisdom, righteousness, sanctification and redemption.*

The exact spiritual words that the Apostle to the nations applies in his gospel are meant to explain each portion Paul delivers in his letters.

> *[11] For what man knoweth the things of a man, save the spirit of man which is in him? even so the things of God knoweth no man, but the Spirit of God.*
>
> *[12] Now we have received, not the spirit of the world, but the spirit which is of God; that we might know the things that are freely given to us of God.*
>
> *[13] Which things also we speak, not in the words which man's wisdom teacheth, but which the Holy Ghost teacheth; comparing spiritual things with spiritual. I Corinthians 2:11-13*

The world system teaches the things that are worldly, having no spiritual value. The wisdom of man is vanity, empty of any truth.

Paul's gospel, on the other hand, contains spiritual truth of the highest value obtainable to those who are spiritually minded. The mysteries revealed in his letters were unattainable until the Lord revealed to him.

> *[1] Let a man so account of us, as of the ministers of Christ, and stewards of the mysteries of God.*
>
> *[2] Moreover it is required in stewards, that a man be found faithful.*
>
> *[3] But with me it is a very small thing that I should be judged of you, or of man's judgment: yea, I judge not mine own self.*

> *⁴For I know nothing by myself; yet am I not hereby justified: but he that judgeth me is the Lord.*
>
> *⁵Therefore judge nothing before the time, until the Lord come, who both will bring to light the hidden things of darkness, and will make manifest the counsels of the hearts: and then shall every man have praise of God. I Corinthians 4:1-5*

There lived no person, prior to Paul's conversion, who knew and understood the *mysteries of God*. Consequently, he realized that his calling was of the highest order. There may be many ministers of Christ but how many among them can call themselves faithful stewards of *the mysteries?* The members of His body will not know until the Lord comes.

Paul also recognized that as he faithfully fulfilled his calling, his authority in the body was magnified. He was capable of exercising necessary apostolic judgment to disobedient members. One such rebellious man in the Corinth ecclesia received from Paul censure and judgment as the overall body was overlooking his sin to Paul's dismay.

> *¹It is reported commonly that there is fornication among you, and such fornication as is not so much as named among the Gentiles, that one should have his father's wife.*
>
> *²And ye are puffed up, and have not rather mourned, that he that hath done this deed might be taken away from among you.*
>
> *³For I verily, as absent in body, but present in spirit, have judged already, as though I were present, concerning him that hath so done this deed,*
>
> *⁴In the name of our Lord Jesus Christ, when ye are gathered together, and my spirit, with the power of our Lord Jesus Christ,*

> [5]To deliver such an one unto Satan for the destruction of the flesh, that the spirit may be saved in the day of the Lord Jesus.
>
> [6]Your glorying is not good. Know ye not that a little leaven leaveneth the whole lump?
>
> [7]Purge out therefore the old leaven, that ye may be a new lump, as ye are unleavened. For even Christ our passover is sacrificed for us: I Corinthians 5:1-7

As he dispensed his gospel to the churches both in person and through letters, Paul was always aware of his audience, adjusting his delivery so as to gain some of them for salvation.

> [16]For though I preach the gospel, I have nothing to glory of: for necessity is laid upon me; yea, woe is unto me, if I preach not the gospel!
>
> [17]For if I do this thing willingly, I have a reward: but if against my will, a dispensation of the gospel is committed unto me.
>
> [18]What is my reward then? Verily that, when I preach the gospel, I may make the gospel of Christ without charge, that I abuse not my power in the gospel.
>
> [19]For though I be free from all men, yet have I made myself servant unto all, that I might gain the more.
>
> [20]And unto the Jews I became as a Jew, that I might gain the Jews; to them that are under the law, as under the law, that I might gain them that are under the law;
>
> [21]To them that are without law, as without law, (being not without law to God, but under the law to Christ,) that I might gain them that are without law. I Corinthians 9:16-23

> *²²To the weak became I as weak, that I might gain the weak: I am made all things to all men, that I might by all means save some.*
>
> *²³And this I do for the gospel's sake, that I might be partaker thereof with you.*

A vital concern of Paul was that the members of the body remember the Lord's death, celebrating His last supper as often as they came together. To this end, he gave specific instructions that he received directly from the Lord.

> *²³For I have received of the Lord that which also I delivered unto you, that the Lord Jesus the same night in which he was betrayed took bread:*
>
> *²⁴And when he had given thanks, he brake it, and said, Take, eat: this is my body, which is broken for you: this do in remembrance of me.*
>
> *²⁵After the same manner also he took the cup, when he had supped, saying, this cup is the new testament in my blood: this do ye, as oft as ye drink it, in remembrance of me.*
>
> *²⁶For as often as ye eat this bread, and drink this cup, ye do shew the Lord's death till he come.*
>
> *²⁷Wherefore whosoever shall eat this bread, and drink this cup of the Lord, unworthily, shall be guilty of the body and blood of the Lord.*
>
> *²⁸But let a man examine himself, and so let him eat of that bread, and drink of that cup. I Corinthians 11:23-28*

The bread, representing Christ's body along with the wine, representing His blood, were the symbols of His *death*. The Lord directed Paul that the ceremony is to be held often. This observance may be the ongoing reality of that which the Lord spoke to His disciples concerning the lady with the alabaster box of precious ointment.

> *⁷There came unto him a woman having an alabaster box of very precious ointment, and poured it on his head, as he sat at meat.*
>
> *⁸But when his disciples saw it, they had indignation, saying, To what purpose is this waste?*
>
> *⁹For this ointment might have been sold for much, and given to the poor.*
>
> *¹⁰When Jesus understood it, he said unto them, Why trouble ye the woman? for she hath wrought a good work upon me.*
>
> *¹¹For ye have the poor always with you; but me ye have not always.*
>
> *¹²For in that she hath poured this ointment on my body, she did it for my burial. Matthew 26:7-12*

Jesus instructed the disciples to make mention of the woman's magnanimous gesture wherever and whenever the gospel is preached.

> *¹³Verily I say unto you, Wheresoever this gospel shall be preached in the whole world, there shall also this, that this woman hath done, be told for a memorial of her. Matthew 26:13*

Jesus recognized no other person in the manner in which he spoke of her sacrifice. He is instruction His disciples concerning His death.

Likewise, in Paul's instructions to the believers at Corinth as well as all of those who hear Paul's gospel throughout the present age, they are to observe the message of Christ's death as represented in the communion supper.

The message in both observances focus on His death.

The instructions in I Corinthians 11 point directly to the fifteenth chapter where Paul summarizes his gospel.

> *¹Moreover, brethren, I declare unto you the gospel which I preached unto you, which also ye have received, and wherein ye stand;*
>
> *²By which also ye are saved, if ye keep in memory what I preached unto you, unless ye have believed in vain.*
>
> *³For I delivered unto you first of all that which I also received, how that Christ died for our sins according to the scriptures;*
>
> *⁴And that he was buried, and that he rose again the third day according to the scriptures:*
>
> *⁵And that he was seen of Cephas, then of the twelve:*
>
> *⁶After that, he was seen of above five hundred brethren at once; of whom the greater part remain unto this present, but some are fallen asleep.*
>
> *⁷After that, he was seen of James; then of all the apostles. I Corinthians 15:1-7*

Three critical gospel points are summarized as Paul presents it to the ecclesia at Corintth. The "bullet points" should be stated any time his gospel is preached.

1.) 3b *<u>Christ died for our sins</u> according to the scriptures;*
2.) 4a *And that <u>he was buried,</u>*
3.) 4b *and that <u>he rose again</u> the third day according to the scripture*

> *¹²Now if Christ be preached that he rose from the dead, how say some among you that there is no resurrection of the dead?*
>
> *¹³But if there be no resurrection of the dead, then is Christ not risen:*
>
> *¹⁴And if Christ be not risen, then is our preaching vain, and your faith is also vain.*
>
> *¹⁵Yea, and we are found false witnesses of God; because we have testified of God that he raised up Christ: whom he raised not up, if so be that the dead rise not.*
>
> *¹⁶For if the dead rise not, then is not Christ raised:*
>
> *¹⁷And if Christ be not raised, your faith is vain; ye are yet in your sins.*
>
> *¹⁸Then they also which are fallen asleep in Christ are perished. I Corinthians 15:12-18*

There are two groups of believers; one group has *fallen asleep in Christ*, other group are those remain alive until he comes.

> *¹⁹If in this life only we have hope in Christ, we are of all men most miserable.*
>
> *²⁰But now is Christ risen from the dead, and become the firstfruits of them that slept.*
>
> *²¹For since by man came death, by man came also the resurrection of the dead.*
>
> *²²For as in Adam all die, even so in Christ shall all be made alive.*

> ²³*But every man in his own order: Christ the firstfruits; afterward they that are Christ's at his coming.*
>
> ²⁴*Then cometh the end, when he shall have delivered up the kingdom to God, even the Father; when he shall have put down all rule and all authority and power.*
>
> ²⁵*For he must reign, till he hath put all enemies under his feet.*
>
> ²⁶*The last enemy that shall be destroyed is death*
>
> ²⁷*For he hath put all things under his feet. But when he saith all things are put under him, it is manifest that he is excepted, which did put all things under him.*
>
> ²⁸*And when all things shall be subdued unto him, then shall the Son also himself be subject unto him that put all things under him, that God may be all in all. I Corinthians 15:19-28*

In the previous verses, Paul's account of the resurrection is the most concise and precise that can be found in all of scripture. As previously stated, he received his gospel and the explanation of spiritual truth in his letters directly from the Lord Jesus Christ.

Here in I Corinthians 15 the three groups or companies to be resurrected are; Christ, the first fruit, they which are his at His coming, and the remainder of humanity at the consummation.

The second group are the members of the body of Christ consisting of the ones, in Christ, that have died and the ones, in Christ, that are alive at His coming.

His explanation of resurrection continues.

> ³⁵*But some man will say, How are the dead raised up? and with what body do they come?*
>
> ³⁶*Thou fool, that which thou sowest is not quickened, except it die:*
>
> ³⁷*And that which thou sowest, thou sowest not that body that shall be, but bare grain, it may chance of wheat, or of some other grain:*
>
> ³⁸*But God giveth it a body as it hath pleased him, and to every seed his own body.*
>
> ³⁹*All flesh is not the same flesh: but there is one kind of flesh of men, another flesh of beasts, another of fishes, and another of birds.*
>
> ⁴⁰*There are also celestial bodies, and bodies terrestrial: but the glory of the celestial is one, and the glory of the terrestrial is another.*
>
> ⁴¹*There is one glory of the sun, and another glory of the moon, and another glory of the stars: for one star differeth from another star in glory.*
>
> ⁴²*So also is the resurrection of the dead. It is sown in corruption; it is raised in incorruption:*
>
> ⁴³*It is sown in dishonour; it is raised in glory: it is sown in weakness; it is raised in power:*
>
> ⁴⁴*It is sown a natural body; it is raised a spiritual body. There is a natural body, and there is a spiritual body. I Corinthians 15:35-44*

All humans, when alive on the earth, are clothed with physical bodies made of the dust of the earth. We live in jars of clay made of earthen material. Within our bodies that are fashioned after Adam, the prototype human, both sin and death affect and hinder the flesh in countless ways.

Upon entry into the state of death, Paul describes the outer body to a seed. When placed in the earth, the outer shell of the seed, subject to the effects of death, withers and deteriorates.

The seed must die followed by new life that springs forth. The seed becomes clothed in a new body from God in a form and fashion that pleases Him.

Paul turns his gaze away from earthly issues, focusing on the glory that exudes from other types of bodies both terrestrial and celestial. The glory of the bodies in each realm differs one from another.

He describes the first body that is of the earth, as it is terrestrial. The next body is of heaven, celestial.

Narrowing his discussion to the resurrection of the dead, Paul teaches that the corpse is sown in corruption, dishonor, weakness, as it is a natural body.

It is raised in incorruption, glory, and power, as it is a spiritual body.

> *⁴⁵And so it is written, The first man Adam was made a living soul; the last Adam was made a quickening spirit.*
>
> *⁴⁶Howbeit that was not first which is spiritual, but that which is natural; and afterward that which is spiritual.*
>
> *⁴⁷The first man is of the earth, earthy; the second man is the Lord from heaven.*
>
> *⁴⁸As is the earthy, such are they also that are earthy: and as is the heavenly, such are they also that are heavenly.*
>
> *⁴⁹And as we have borne the image of the earthy, we shall also bear the image of the heavenly. I Corinthians 15:45-49*

Adam was the first man. He was the natural man, before all others. He was soulish, influenced by desires.

Jesus Christ, as the last Adam, represented all of humanity as He suffered, was nailed to the cross, died and was placed as a corpse into the tomb. He became *a quickening spirit,* the one who will give life to all who go into death.

Adam, as the first man, was made of the earth, soilish.

Jesus Christ is the second man, our *Lord from heaven.*

As humans, of Adam's race, *we have borne the image of the earthy.*

As being *in Christ, we shall also bear the image of the heavenly*

> *⁵⁰Now this I say, brethren, that flesh and blood cannot inherit the kingdom of God; neither doth corruption inherit incorruption.*
>
> *⁵¹Behold, I shew you a mystery; We shall not all sleep, but we shall all be changed,*
>
> *⁵²In a moment, in the twinkling of an eye, at the last trump: for the trumpet shall sound, and the dead shall be raised incorruptible, and we shall be changed.*
>
> *⁵³For this corruptible must put on incorruption, and this mortal must put on immortality. I Corinthians 15:50-53*

Paul was a steward of the *mysteries of God.* Jesus imparted into him a treasury of mysteries, which are secrets of God unknown to no man until revealed to Paul. The mysteries were unveiled by Paul through his letters, becoming a integral part of his gospel.

Of paramount importance, Paul in Romans 5:11 disclosed that the members of Christ' body, the ecclesia of God, were to receive a special gift, which he used Greek word, *katallage*. As discussed previously in this manuscript, God has completely changed His relationship with humanity by means of the *conciliation,* which is accomplished in *the death of His Son.*

The complete and total change, expressed by the crucifixion of Jesus, whereby the *old humanity* was crucified together with Him, followed by His new life and resurrection, whereby the *new humanity* was created in Him, is a foundational truth in Paul's gospel. All believers are to receive this truth as a spiritual gift.

> *And not only so, but we also joy in God through our Lord Jesus Christ, by whom we have now received the atonement (katallage). Romans 5:11*

The conciliation is a spiritual truth that is to be included in the gospel of Paul wherever it is proclaimed. The mystery cited above in *I Corinthians 15:51* describes the culmination of the change when our terrestrial bodies will become celestial bodies.

Paul announces that the change in our bodies will occur will occur instantly.

> [52]*In a moment, in the twinkling of an eye, at the last trump: for the trumpet shall sound, and the dead shall be raised incorruptible, and we shall be changed.*
>
> [53]*For this corruptible must put on incorruption, and this mortal must put on immortality. I Corinthians 15:52-53*

The Body of Christ will be snatched up in the air to be joined to Christ, as the Head of the Body. This current eon will be brought to a close, the next eon will be ushered in.

> ⁵⁴*So when this corruptible shall have put on incorruption, and this mortal shall have put on immortality, then shall be brought to pass the saying that is written, Death is swallowed up in victory.*
>
> ⁵⁵*O death, where is thy sting? O grave, where is thy victory?*
>
> ⁵⁶*The sting of death is sin; and the strength of sin is the law.*
>
> ⁵⁷*But thanks be to God, which giveth us the victory through our Lord Jesus Christ.*
>
> ⁵⁸*Therefore, my beloved brethren, be ye stedfast, unmoveable, always abounding in the work of the Lord, forasmuch as ye know that your labour is not in vain in the Lord. I Corinthians15:45-58*

This final section of I Corinthians, chapter 15, describes the wondrous event that this manuscript discloses; the manifestation of the sons of God. It is also known as the Son-placing or Sonship.

As humanity approaches the end of this age, the members of the body of Christ, the church, are to embrace the truths of Paul's gospel. The Holy Spirit of God will equip and lead the Body out of a minority status to the mature status of God's sons. The Body will be prepared to enter the administration of the Kingdom in the heavenly realms along with the nation of Israel on the earth.

The Lord, in the special prayer He taught the disciples, asked the Father to send His Kingdom from above, that His will be done on earth as it is in heaven.

The fulfillment of that prayer will be realized in the age to come, and beyond.

CHAPTER 8

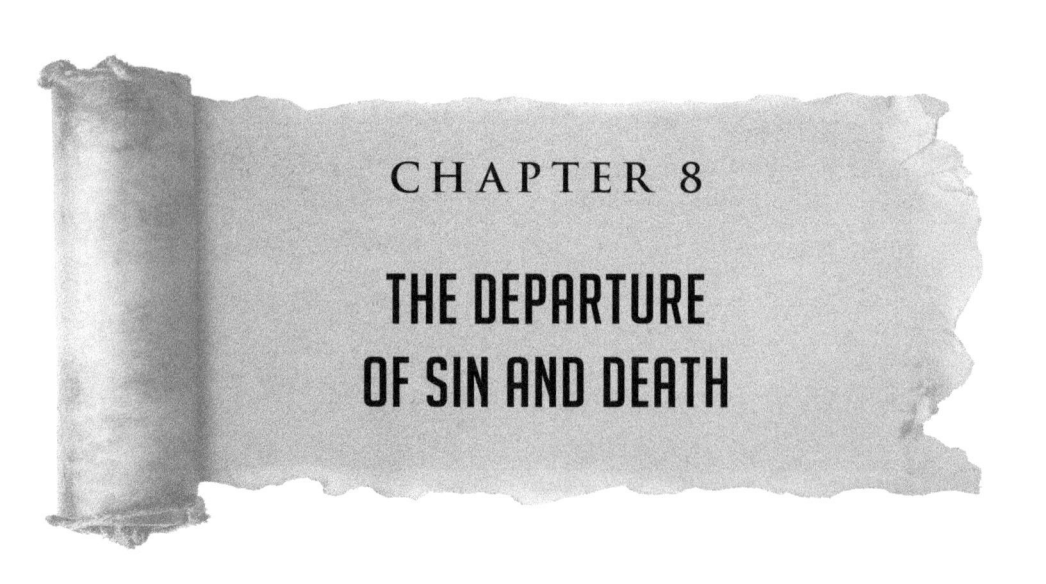

THE DEPARTURE OF SIN AND DEATH

THE EONIAN PLAN OF THE RESTITUTION OF ALL THINGS

The Apostle Peter, as he was explaining to the Jewish throng on the day of Pentecost when God poured out His spirit upon them, sought to inform them about Jesus' mission during His first visitation. He then spoke to them concerning the Lord's next return.

> *Repent ye therefore, and be converted, that your sins may be blotted out when the times of refreshing shall come from the presence of the Lord.*
>
> *He will send Jesus Christ, who was previously preached to you: Whom the heavens must receive until the times of restitution of all things, which God hath spoken by the mouth of all his holy prophets since the world began. Acts 3:19-21*

And he continued to address them concerning the fulfillment of God's covenant with Abraham.

> *Ye are the children of the prophets, and of the covenant which God made with our fathers, saying unto Abraham, And in thy seed shall all the kindreds of the earth be blessed.*
>
> *Unto you first, God, having raised up his Son Jesus, sent him to bless you by turning away every one of you from his iniquities. Acts 3:25-26*

The restoration of all things is promised in the Scripture. This is the Father's glorious work through His Son, the Lord. Jesus will remain in heaven *until the time of the restitution of all things.* The word *restitution (apokatastasis, Strong's #G605, reconstitution)* has been an expectation of Israel since the time of the prophets. The disciples of Christ, at the time of His ascent back to heaven, voiced their question concerning this promise as it concerned the nation of Israel.

> *When they therefore came together, they asked of him, saying, Lord, wilt thou at this time restore again the kingdom to Israel?*
>
> *And he said unto them, It is not for you to know the times or the seasons, which the Father hath put in his own power.*
>
> *But ye shall receive power; after that, that the Holy Ghost will come upon you; and ye shall be witnesses unto me both in Jerusalem and in all Judaea and in Samaria, and unto the uttermost part of the earth.*
>
> *And when he had spoken these things, while they beheld, he was taken up, and a cloud received him out of their sight.*
>
> *And while they looked steadfastly toward heaven as he went up, behold, two men stood by them in white apparel.*
>
> *Which also said, Ye men of Galilee, why stand ye gazing up into heaven? This same Jesus, who is taken up from you into heaven, shall so come in like manner as ye have seen him go into heaven. Acts 1:6-11*

The restoration of all things is promised in the Scripture. This is the Father's glorious work through His Son, the Lord Jesus, who will remain in heaven *until the time of the restitution of all things*. The word *restitution (apokatastasis, Strong's #G605, reconstitution)* has been an expectation of Israel since the time of the prophets. The disciples of Christ, at the time of His ascent back to heaven, voiced their question concerning this promise as it concerned the nation of Israel.

> *And Jesus said unto them: Verily, I say unto you, That ye which have followed me, in the regeneration when the Son of man shall sit on the throne of his glory, ye also shall sit upon twelve thrones, judging the twelve tribes of Israel. Matthew 19:28*

Regeneration will characterize Israel's national new birth.

Paul, as the apostle to the nations, used this same word (*palingenesia, Strong's #G3824, spiritual renovation*) when he wrote to Titus.

> *For we, ourselves, were sometimes foolish, disobedient, deceived, serving divers lusts and pleasures, living in malice and envy, hateful, and hating one another.*
>
> *But after that, the kindness and love of God, our Saviour, toward man appeared.*
>
> *Not by works of righteousness which we have done, but according to his mercy, he saved us, by the washing of regeneration and renewing of the Holy Ghost;*
>
> *Which he shed on us abundantly through Jesus Christ, our Saviour;*
>
> *That being justified by his grace, we should be made heirs according to the hope of eternal life. Titus 3:3-7*

Jesus will reign when He returns to earth. His reign will last a day on God's calendar, which is 1,000 years, as Peter testified.

> *But, beloved, be not ignorant of this one thing: that one day is with the Lord as a thousand years, and a thousand years as one day. II Peter 3:8*

We are presently awaiting the day of His return, which is known to His body, the church, as the Day of Christ. While we wait, the church is actively preparing for the Day of Christ, as described by Paul in the following verses.

> *So that ye come behind in no gift, waiting for the coming of our Lord Jesus Christ, who shall also confirm you unto the end, that ye may be blameless in the day of our Lord Jesus Christ. I Corinthians 1:7-8*

Paul also spoke of the Day of Christ to the church in Philippi.

> *I thank my God for every remembrance of you.*
>
> *Always in every prayer of mine for you all, making requests with joy,*
>
> *For your fellowship in the gospel from the first day until now,*
>
> *Being confident of this very thing, that he who hath begun a good work in you will perform it until the day of Jesus Christ:*
>
> *Even as it is meet for me to think this of you all, because I have you in my heart, inasmuch as both in my bonds and in the defense and confirmation of the gospel, ye all are partakers of my grace.*
>
> *For God is my record, how greatly I long after you all in the bowels of Jesus Christ.*

> *And this I pray, that your love may abound yet more and more in knowledge and in all judgement;*
>
> *That ye may approve things that are excellent; that ye may be sincere and without offense till the day of Christ. Philippians 1:3-10*

Paul encourages believers to narrow their focus as the day of Christ approaches. Concentrate on matters of surpassing importance that Paul reveals in his letters, being on the finished work of Christ.

We are not to be anxious about it, hoping the day comes quickly and rescues us from a failing world, as Paul counseled the church at Thessalonica.

> *Finally, brethren, pray for us that the word of the Lord may have free course and be glorified, even as it is with you:*
>
> *And that we may be delivered from unreasonable and wicked men, for all men have no faith.*
>
> *But the Lord is faithful, who shall establish you and keep you from evil.*
>
> *And we have confidence in the Lord touching you that ye both do and will do the things that we command you to do.*
>
> *And the Lord directs your hearts into the love of God and into the patient waiting for Christ. II Thessalonians 3:1 –5*

When He returns, He will reign as King of Kings and Lord of Lords.

The adversary will be chained for 1,000 years.

> *And I saw an angel come down from heaven, having the key to the bottomless pit and a great chain in his hand.*

> *And he laid hold on the dragon, that old serpent, which is the Devil, and Satan, and bound him for a thousand years.*
>
> *And cast him into the bottomless pit, and shut him up, and set a seal upon him, that he should deceive the nations no more, till the thousand years should be fulfilled, and after that he must be loosed a little season. Revelation 20:1-3*

The lies and deceptions of the prince of the power of the air will be reined in. The truth will begin to be proclaimed in an unhindered manner. It will be received with gladness by those who are called. It will, however, continue to be rejected by those in whom the law of sin and death reigns in the flesh.

The delusion of humanity in these last days has been slowly progressing, like the rising tide. But of late, with the conflicting influences of oppressing governments coupled with the sleight of hand of media outlets that cannot be trusted to disseminate truth, a feeling of hopelessness seeks to cripple the faith of even the elect. But He will cut short this opposition at the proper time.

The masses have embraced the strong delusion of the last days, which will overtake those who have not received the love of truth described by Paul. *And with all deceivableness and unrighteousness in them that perish because they received not <u>the love of the truth</u>, that they might be saved.*

> *And for this cause, God shall send them strong delusions that they should believe a lie.*
>
> *That they all might be damned who believed not the truth but had pleasure in unrighteousness. II Thessalonians 2:10-12*

It is the love of God that flows out of the truth that the ungodly do not receive from Him. It is not just any truth that conveys this love, but the truth announced in Paul's gospel. The gospel truth is the source of love.

God has created and established in Christ an entirely new humanity. The initial company of this new creation has been elected and called since the time of Christ's ministry on earth until now and will be finalized up to the time of His return.

The new humanity cannot sin and will not die. At present, the new humanity (*kainos anthropos*) exists in the spiritual realm of Christ. When He returns, the new humanity will exist in bodily form, with Christ as the head of the body.

As the body of Christ awaits His return, an essential element of Paul's gospel presents the truth of the new man, which believers are to receive, believe in, and convey to others. It is important for all believers to embrace the ministry that Paul describes in II Corinthians 5.

> *Therefore, if any man be in Christ, he is a new creature: old things are passed away; behold, all things are made new.*
>
> *And all things are of God, who hath reconciled us to himself by Jesus Christ and hath given to us the ministry of reconciliation;*
>
> *To wit, that God was in Christ, reconciling the world unto himself, not imputing their trespasses unto them, and hath committed unto us the word of reconciliation. II Corinthians 5:17-19*

Two major conditions affect all of humanity during this time of the completion of this eon: a great falling away and the ministry of reconciliation of the Body of Christ.

This great falling away is in accord with the unspiritual condition of humanity Paul spoke of in his second letter to Thessalonica, which characterizes this evil age.

> *We also know that in the last days, perilous times will come. For men shall be lovers of their own selves, covetous, boasters, proud, blasphemers, disobedient to parents, unthankful, unholy,*
>
> *Without natural affection, truce breakers, false accusers, incontinent, fierce, despisers of those that are good,*
>
> *Traitors, heady, high-minded, lovers of pleasures more than lovers of God;*
>
> *Having a form of godliness but denying the power thereof: from such turn away. II Timothy 3:1-5*

Paul painstakingly informed us of these grave matters through his spiritual son, Timothy.

A tsunami of deception has replaced the slowly moving tide of ungodliness upon the earth. The dishonesty and trickery of the rulers of this age, both in the spiritual realm as well as the human realm are ever-advancing to a climax. When Jesus returns, both the reconstituted nation of Israel and the Body of Christ will join the captain of their salvation in a joint crusade of spiritual warfare against the kingdom of darkness. Israel's battles in Canaan Land were a precursor to the warfare that lies ahead.

The triumph in this warfare will be championed by the King of kings, and the Lord of lords.

As this current era continues towards its consummation, in its final days, the ungodly will continue to descend into greater rebellion against God and against Christ. Paul warned of the treacherous time.

The unbelieving masses in their outward false religious service will be exposed, as Paul described, *"Having a form of godliness but denying the power thereof: from such turn away."*

During this current age, the *penalty of sin* is nullified by faith in the shed blood of Jesus, which covers over the sins of the one confessing faith in His blood. Also, in this time in which the Body of Christ is to join Christ in His victory over sin, *the power of sin* is nullified by the joint crucifixion with Him proclaimed in Paul's gospel. At the time of the glorious manifestation of God's sons, *the presence of sin* that masters over the Old Humanity will not affect the bodies of the New Man.

The New Man is to conduct the ministry of reconciliation by proclaiming the truth of the total change that God has accomplished through His Son, the Lord Jesus Christ. Believers are entreated to take to themselves the truth of the change that Paul first announced in Roman 5.

> *And not only so, but we also find joy in God through our Lord Jesus Christ, by whom we have now received the atonement. Romans 5:11*

This companion truth is separate from the justification for the covering of sins through Christ's blood. The grandeur of the reconciliation is obscured by the translation of *katallage* as *atonement*. The truth of *katallage* reveals that God has totally changed humanity from the old to the new. The old humanity was put to death in Christ on the cross when He was crucified (Romans 6:6); the new humanity came into existence in Christ in His resurrection.

Believers are instructed by Paul to *put off the old man and put on the new.*

> *Having abolished in his flesh the enmity, even the law of commandments contained in ordinances; for to make in himself of twain one new man, so making peace; Ephesians 2:15*

And also,

> *That ye put off concerning the former conversation the old man, which is corrupt according to the deceitful lusts, and be renewed in the spirit of your mind; and that ye put on the new man, which after God is created in righteousness and true holiness. Ephesians 4:22-24*

And also,

> *Lie not one to another, seeing that ye have put off the old man with his deeds; Colossians 3:9*

The displacement of the old humanity and the replacement of the new humanity are to be realized by the body of Christ as expressions of faith as the dusk of the current era draws to a close and the daybreak of the new age advances.

In the next age, not only will the Body of Christ, as the New Man, inhabit new bodies, but Israel, as God's chosen nation on earth, will also be in a new relationship with God. He promises a new covenant will be established (Jer. 31:31, Heb. 8:8, 8:13, 12:24) with the chosen nation. This will establish Israel's divine service to God through God's new covenant with them. Their *son placing* (huisthesia) will reestablish the chosen nation with the authority to fulfill their divine calling to present God to the nations of the earth.

In the final days of the restitution of all things, sin and death, the primary weapons of the deceiver of the nations, will be eliminated.

> *For he must reign till he hath put all enemies under his feet.*
>
> *The last enemy that shall be destroyed is death. I Corinthians 15:25-26*

If these verses were a part of the testimony of every believer, all enemies would begin to be subdued, especially *enemies of the cross of Christ (Philippians 3:18)*. But few in the visible church seem to have such a clear and positive witness.

Nevertheless, Christ's overwhelming victory will overcome all adversity and resistance to God's mercy, grace, and love.

The time will come when sin will no longer reign over humanity. Sin will be put away by the universal application of Christ's sacrifice.

> *For then must he often have suffered since the foundation of the world, but now, once at the end of the world, hath he appeared to put away sin by the sacrifice of himself. Hebrews 9:26*

The *putting away* in this verse is the Greek word *athetesis, Strong's #G115, cancellation, or disannulling, or put away.*

The "putting away of sin" is to be realized first in the church, the body of Christ. Paul's gospel clearly establishes this divine truth, as he proclaimed that the *body of sin* is neutralized by the truth in Romans 6:6. Sin is to reign over humanity no longer. Further, at the time of redemption at His appearing, sin will no longer be operating in the new bodies of believers.

And lastly, at the consummation, both sin and death's presence in the creation will end.

An interesting observation concerns the word used twice in this verse, which is "world." As to the *foundation of the world,* the verse is referring to the *kosmos,* the system of the universe. At *the end of the world,* Paul is not referring to the *kosmos,* but is applying the phrase *suntelia, Strong's #4930, the together finish of the eons,* when sin will no longer be evident within God's creation. Sin will be put away, and death will be destroyed, swallowed up in Christ's victory (I Corinthians 15:26).

> *So when this corruptible shall have put on incorruption and this mortal shall have put on immortality, then shall be brought to pass the saying that is written: Death is swallowed up in victory.*
>
> *O death, where is thy sting? O grave, where is thy victory?*
>
> *The sting of death is sin, and the strength of sin is the law. I Corinthians 15:54–56*

Death will be terminated by the lake of fire, as John stated.

> *And death and hell were cast into the lake of fire. This is the second death. Revelation 20:14*

The two enemies of God that entered the world through Adam's disobedience will be rendered totally ineffective by Christ, no longer separating humanity from God. This spiritual fact will be experienced by the Body of Christ in their new bodies when He returns, but it must now be realized by faith in the elements of Paul's gospel.

Both sin and death will continue in this era and will also be present in the age to come because the flesh is hostile to the spirit and the complete message of the cross is not fully proclaimed or believed. Adam's family, into which all humans enter this creation, will continue to be born and die. The Old Humanity will proceed in the Kingdom but will not be directly influenced by Satan, as he will be chained until the end of the millennium approaches.

The lies, the destructive and devious plans, the fear of death, and all manner of evil that the adversary of God exhibits will be reigned in by Christ's victorious reign. As God's Spirit is poured out upon all flesh, humanity will favorably respond to the saving gospel that proclaims and magnifies the Lord's saving work.

When his imprisonment lapses, God and man's chief enemy will be freed to make a final attempt to overcome Israel and gain control of the humanity he once succeeded in seducing, capturing, and dominating.

One last campaign of evil will arise in a Satanic effort to regain the lost domain of darkness. The Kingdom of light will prevail as all authority, rule, and power will be put under Christ's feet (I Corinthians 15:25).

John reported in his final portion of the Revelation of Jesus Christ the consummation of the next age.

> *And I saw an angel come down from heaven, having the key to the bottomless pit and a great chain in his hand.*
>
> *And he laid hold on the dragon, that old serpent, which is the Devil, and Satan, and bound him for a thousand years.*
>
> *And cast him into the bottomless pit, shut him up, and set a seal upon him, that he should deceive the nations no more, till the thousand years should be fulfilled, and after that he must be loosed a little season. Revelation 20:1-3*

John reveals both the beginning and the end of the next age.

> *And I saw thrones, and they sat upon them, and judgment was given unto them: and I saw the souls of them that were beheaded for the witness of Jesus, and for the word of God, and which had not worshipped the beast, neither his image, neither had received his mark upon their foreheads, or in their hands; and they lived and reigned with Christ a thousand years.*
>
> *But the rest of the dead lived not again until the thousand years were finished. This is the first resurrection.*

> *Blessed and holy is he that hath part in the first resurrection: on such the second death hath no power, but they shall be priests of God and of Christ, and shall reign with him a thousand years.*
>
> *And when the thousand years are expired, Satan shall be loosed out of his prison, Revelation 20:4-7*

When the adversary is released from his imprisonment, John describes the rebellion that ensues in Rev 20:8–10.

> *And shall go out to deceive the nations which are in the four quarters of the earth, Gog and Magog, to gather them together to battle: the number of whom is as the sand of the sea.*
>
> *And they went up on the breadth of- earth, and compassed the camp of the saints and the beloved city, and fire came down from God out of heaven and devoured them.*
>
> *And the devil that deceived them was cast into the lake of fire and brimstone, where the beast and the false prophet are, and shall be tormented day and night for ever and ever. Revelation 20:8-10*

Following the putting away of the devil, beast, and false prophet, the dead who were not raised in the first resurrection will be made to stand before God at the great white throne.

> *And I saw a great white throne, and him that sat on it, from whose face the earth and the heaven fled away; and there was found no place for them.*
>
> *And I saw the dead, small and great, stand before God, and the books were opened, and another book was opened, which is the book of life, and the dead were judged out of those things that were written in the books according to their works.*

> *And the sea gave up the dead that were in it, and death and hell delivered up the dead that were in them, and they judged every man according to their works.*
>
> *And death and hell were cast into the lake of fire. This is the second death.*
>
> *And whosoever was not found written in the book of life was cast into the lake of fire. Revelation 20:11-15*

The renovation will then be completed both in heaven and earth, as John describes in the final chapters of the Revelation of Jesus Christ.

The eons will be concluded. The first creation will be replaced by the new creation in Christ.

The New Humanity will replace the Old Humanity. As believers realize the truth of being in Christ, sharing His death, and sharing His life, He will subdue all resistance towards God that is expressed in the children of disobedience (Ephesians 2:2).

Expressing the faith of the newness of life and serving in the newness of spirit are the obedient steps that must now be displayed by the church, the called-out assembly that belongs to Him and is awaiting His return.

As we conclude this manuscript, it is my sincere desire to impart some insight into the words of unity that Paul expressed throughout his letters.

When used as a prefix, the Greek word *sun* is a primary preposition denoting unity. It generally denotes that the root word to which it is joined is presented in a joint manner. As an attachment, I have listed in the appendix those *sun* words discussed in the narrative.

Before closing our discussion, I offer some words used in the Greek text that have the word *sun* attached as a suffix. An example of this is the powerful word *righteousness*. The root of righteousness is *justice*. It pertains to that which is right, equitable, and proper.

God is righteous. Everything He does is right. Nothing He accomplishes is inequitable. It permeates His character and all that He does.

The root word for *righteousness* is *dike (pronounced dee-kay)*, that which is right and just.

Paul first uses the term "righteousness" in the opening chapter of his letter to the Romans. *For I am not ashamed of the gospel of Christ: for it is the power of God unto salvation to every one that believeth; to the Jew first, and also to the Greek.*

> *[17] For therein is the righteousness of God revealed from faith to faith: as it is written, Thee just shall live by faith. Romans 1:16,17*

The gospel contains God's power to save. His righteousness is revealed in the gospel, rendering the one who hears it as being *just*. This is what Abraham discovered. A gospel message was delivered to him, and as he expressed faith in what God said to him, his faith was reckoned unto him as righteousness (Romans 4:1–9). Abraham believed in the God who justifies the ungodly (Romans 4:5).

When God presents to any person the gospel of their salvation through faith in Christ, the same reckoning occurs as that which Abraham received. Abraham and the believing sinner today receive the equitable gift of *righteousness* through the all-sufficient grace of God.

The Greek word for *righteousness* is *dikaiosune,* a compound word of two parts: justice and togetherness, or unification. God actually shares His righteousness with the believer, who, by the grace of God, was once a sinner but is now a saint.

That is why the body of Christ should return to Paul's gospel. It contains the power of God for salvation: sins being covered over by Christ's blood, the power of sin rendered idle by His death on the cross, His new life shared by His resurrection, and the victorious power of the law of the spirit of the life that is in Christ Jesus.

The restoration of the gospel of Paul, the apostle to the nations, is to occur in the church, God's called-out assembly in this age.

Let us be the ones that lead the charge, being joined together as Paul exhorted the saints at Ephesus.

> *That ye put off concerning the former conversation with the old man, which is corrupt according to the deceitful lusts;*
>
> *And be renewed in the spirit of your mind;*
>
> *And that ye put on the new man, who, after God, is created in righteousness and true holiness. Ephesians 4:22-24*

These instructions from Paul, as the Apostle to the Nations, are to be applied to the church, the called-out assembly of believers throughout this eon as it draws to a close. A new eon will soon be entered wherein both the Body of Christ and restored Israel will administer the Kingdom of God with Christ Jesus as the head of the body, and recognized as Israel's Messiah, bringing all rule, authority, and power into subjection.

God, the Father, has placed the eons as a part of His magnificent plan to reveal the glory of His Son, and the family has been brought forth to worship and honor Him.

Also attached to this manuscript as Appendix II is a brief presentation of the times of the eons (chronos aionios) during which God, the Father, through the agency of His Son, the Lord Jesus Christ, will restore all things in the completion of the plan for the ages.

Paul's fitting conclusion of his letter to the Romans is presented as a proper finale to our study together.

> *[25] Now to him that is of power to establish you according to my gospel and the preaching of Jesus Christ, according to the revelation of the mystery, which has been kept secret since the world began,*
>
> *[26] But now it is made manifest, and by the scriptures of the prophets, according to the commandment of the everlasting God, it is made known to all nations for the obedience of faith:*
>
> *[27] To God only wise, be glory through Jesus Christ forever. Amen. Romans 16:25-27*

EPILOGUE

In the year 2020, a twelve-year writing project was completed. The goal was to produce three separate books that commented on Paul's Letter to the Romans. I observed that the Apostle Paul's foundational letter is written in three sections; Romans Chapters 1 to 8, Romans Chapters 9 to 11, and the final section, Romans Chapters 12 to 16.

The first book in the series was Chasing Truth, published in 2009, which focused on Chapters 1-8. In 2017, Paul's unique message of the good news concerning Christ was fully discussed in a revised edition.

The second book, All Israel Shall Be Saved, was published in 2016, in which Paul presented his distinctive and matchless perspective on the nation of Israel's current status and future restoration in Chapters 9 –11. It was revised in 2019.

The most recent book, The Victory of the New Man and the Mysteries of God, was published in 2021, discussing the concluding five chapters of Paul's Romans letter and highlighting the gospel's victory as lived in and through the members of the body of Christ. The Victory volume presents a discourse on service to God and service to others conducted by the members of Christ's body, the church.

The third book brought the Romans project to its proper conclusion. All three of the books were written and published under the pen name Joel Zao.

This current manuscript is presented to expand Paul's distinctive viewpoint of God's plan of salvation through Jesus Christ, His Son. The study focuses on a group of unique words that clarify our relationship with Him and with each other as believers in Christ Jesus, members of His body, the church.

APPENDIX: WORDS OF UNITY IN PAUL'S LETTERS

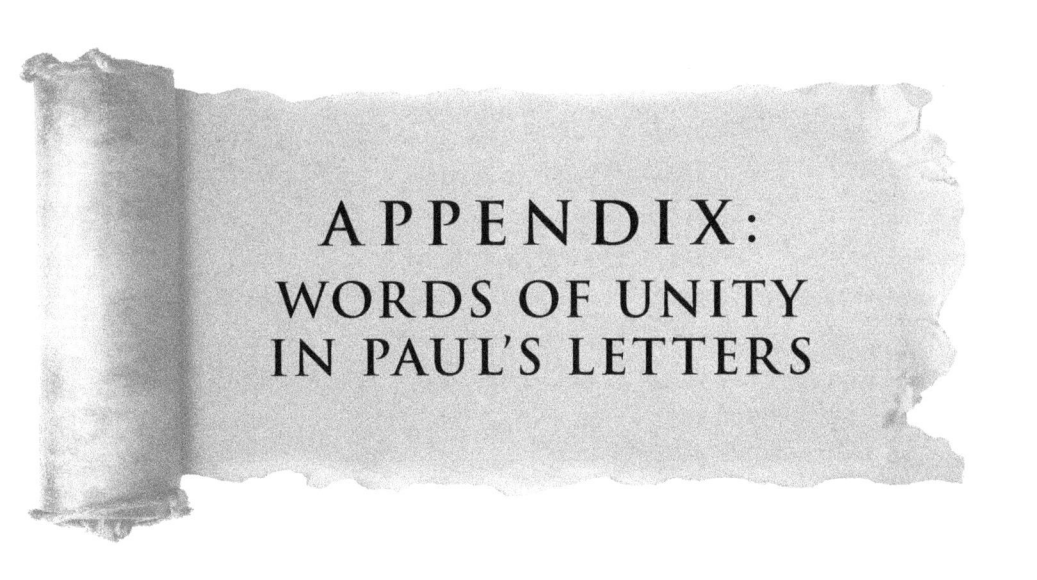

THE "SUN" WORDS

The unique "sun" words Paul utilized in his letters are presented in this manuscript as they appeared in his letters, beginning with his letter to the church in Rome. The following list is not exhaustive but contains the unity words that are presented in the foregoing manuscript.

The words appear in the list in the order that they appear in the text of the chapters of the New Testament scriptures.

The word	*Strong's #*	*Definition*	*Book, chapter, verse*
Those found in Romans:			
Sumparakaleo	G4837	to console jointly	Rom. 1:12
Sunthapto	G4916	to bury jointly	Rom. 6:4
Sumphusos	G4854	born together with	Rom. 6:5
Sustauroo	G4957	crucify together with	Rom. 6:6
Suzao	G4800	live together with	Rom. 6:8
Summartureo	G4828	to jointly testify	Rom. 8:16, 9:1
Sunkleronomos	G4789	joint heirs	Rom. 8:17

Sunpascho	*G4841*	*suffer together with*	*Rom. 8:17*
Sundoxazo	*G4888*	*glorified together*	*Rom. 8:17*
Sustenazo	*G4959*	*to moan jointly*	*Rom. 8:22*
Sunodino	*G4944*	*birth pains together*	*Rom. 8:22*
Sunantilambanomai	*G4878*	*cooperate together*	*Rom. 8:26*
Sunergeo	*G4903*	*work together with*	*Rom. 8:28*
Summorphos	*G4832*	*jointly formed*	*Rom. 8:29*
Sunteleo	*G4931*	*to end together*	*Rom. 9:28*
Suntemno	*G4932*	*do concisely with*	*Rom. 9:28*
Sunkampto	*G4781*	*to bend together*	*Rom. 11:10*
Sunkoinonos	*G4791*	*a co-participant*	*Rom. 11:17*
Sunkleio	*G4788*	*to shut together*	*Rom. 11:32*
Sumboulos	*G4825*	*to counsel with*	*Rom. 11:34*
Suschematizo	*G4964*	*conform to*	*Rom. 12:2*
Sunapago	*G4879*	*to take off together*	*Rom. 12:16*

Those found in I Corinthians:

Sugkrino	*G4793*	*matching two things together*	*I Cor. 2:13*
Sumbibazo	*G4822*	*deducing together*	*I Cor. 2:16*
Sunergos	*G4904*	*working together*	*I Cor. 3:9*
Sumbasileuo	*G4821*	*reigning together*	*I Cor. 4:8*
Suneideis	*G4893*	*the conscience*	*I Cor. 10:25*
Sunerchomai	*G4905*	*to assemble*	*I Cor. 11:17*
Sugkerannumi	*G4786*	*to mix together*	*I Cor. 12:24*

Those found in II Corinthians:

Sumphonesis	*G4857*	*agreement*	*II Cor. 6:15*
Sugkatathesis	*G4783*	*concurrence*	*II Cor. 6:16*
Sunapothenesko	*G4880*	*to die together*	*II Cor. 7:3*
Suzao	*G4800*	*to live together*	*II Cor. 7:3*
Sunekdemos	*G4898*	*fellow-traveller*	*II Cor. 8:19*
Sunergos	*G4904*	*fellow-worker*	*II Cor. 8:19*
Sugkrino	*G4793*	*comparing*	*II Cor. 10:12*
Sunapostello	*G4882*	*dispatch together*	*II Cor. 12:18*

Those found in Galatians:

Sumparalambano	G4838	take along together	Gal. 2:1
Sunapago	G4879	led away together with	Gal. 2:13
Sustauroo	G4957	to be crucified together	Ga. 2:20

Those found in Ephesians:

Suzoopoieo	G4806	to reanimate conjointly with	Eph. 2:5
Sunegeiro	G4891	rouses together with	Eph. 2:6
Sugkathizo	G4776	to seat in company with	Eph. 2:6
Sumpolites	G4847	citizens together with	Eph. 2:19
Sunarmologeo	G4883	close-jointed together	Eph. 2:21
Sunoikodomeo	G4925	built together	Eph. 2:22
Sugkleronomos	G4789	co-heirs	Eph. 3:6
Sussomos	G4954	a joint body	Eph. 3:6
Summetochos	G4830	joint partakers (of promise)	Eph. 3:6
Sundesmos	G4886	a together bond	Eph. 4:3
Sunarmologeo	G4883	to be framed (joined) together	Eph. 4:16
Sumbibazo	G4822	knit together	Eph. 4:16
Summetochos	G4830	joint partakers (of indignation)	Eph. 5:7
Sugkoinoneo	G4790	joint partaker of	Eph. 5:11

Those found in Philippians:

Sugkoinonos	G4791	a co-participant	Phil. 1:7
Sumparameno	G4839	to remain in company with	Phil. 1:25
Sunathleo	G4866	to compete together with	Phil. 1:27
Sumpsupchos	G4861	co-spirited (like-minded)	Phil. 2:2
Sugchairo	G4796	to rejoice together	Phil. 2:17

The "sun" words contained throughout most of Paul's thirteen letters were utilized by the apostle to set apart his distinctly original gospel.

As Paul explained in his letter to the Galatians that no one revealed the secrets he presented. He received the secrets through revelation to him directly from the Lord Jesus Christ.

Milton Keynes UK
Ingram Content Group UK Ltd.
UKHW012152090624
443713UK00001B/129